GASTRIC SLEEVE BARIATRIC COOKBOOK

GASTRIC SLEEVE BARIATRIC COOKBOOK

The content contained within this book may not be reproduced, duplicated or transmitted without direct written permission from the author or the publisher.

Under no circumstances will any blame or legal responsibility be held against the publisher, or author, for any damages, reparation, or monetary loss due to the information contained within this book. Either directly or indirectly.

Legal Notice:

This book is copyright protected. This book is only for personal use. You cannot amend, distribute, sell, use, quote or paraphrase any part, or the content within this book, without the consent of the author or publisher.

Disclaimer Notice:

Please note the information contained within this document is for educational and entertainment purposes only. All effort has been executed to present accurate, up to date, and reliable, complete information. No warranties of any kind are declared or implied. Readers acknowledge that the author is not engaging in the rendering of legal, financial, medical or professional advice. The content within this book has been derived from various sources. Please consult a licensed professional before attempting any techniques outlined in this book.

By reading this document, the reader agrees that under no circumstances is the author responsible for any losses, direct or indirect, which are incurred as a result of the use of information contained within this document, including, but not limited to, — errors, omissions, or inaccuracies.

Copyright @ 2023 by

Printed in United States of America
10 9 8 7 6 5 4

This book is dedicated to the weight-loss surgery community who continue to inspire me every day.

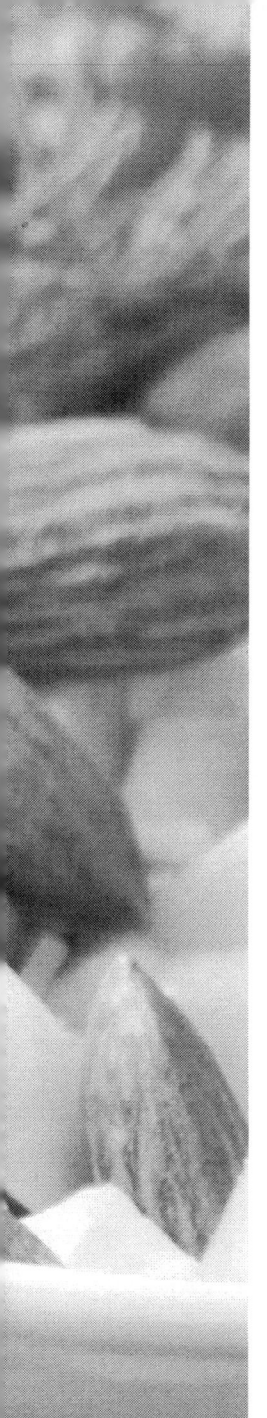

CONTENTS

8	Introduction
9	Part 1: All About Gastric Sleeve
13	Part 2: Your New Life Style
21	Part 3: Full Liquid Foods
27	Part 4: Pureed Food
35	Part 5: Soft Foods
42	Part 6: Breakfasts
50	Part 7: Soups and Stews
57	Part 8: Vegetables and Sides
63	Part 9: Poultry
70	Part 10: Pork, Beef and Lamb
75	Part 11: Fish and Seafood
82	Part 12: Desserts
89	Part 13: Staples, Sauces

INTRODUCTION

In the past 5 years in the United States, gastric sleeve surgery has tripled. This gastroectomy technique has become very popular. Bariatric surgery is a great tool for those with obesity, those with obesity-related health problems, and people who want to lose a significant amount of weight in a short time. Any kind of bariatric surgery, whether gastric sleeve or other, is a tool that can change your life.

In order to be successful after this surgery, the key is to follow specific dietary guidelines. In this book, you will find the right strategies to definitely succeed both physically and psychologically, and more importantly, you will not only be thinner, but you will learn how to have a healthy and happy life.

If you have done a google search surely you have found millions of diverse information and felt lost and confused. I wrote this cookbook so that I could give people a simple guide on what to eat and what to avoid after surgery.

If you have had a gastric sleeve I want to make sure that you have no doubt about what, when, and how much to eat. This book is meant to be not only a cookbook but more importantly a guide for how to eat from the first day of surgery until your millionth day.

And now, let me congratulate you, you have finally decided to take charge of your health and your life. You know you can do it and you will succeed. You deserve to feel lighter, more energetic, and healthier.

Come on, let's get started!

PART ONE

ALL ABOUT GASTRIC SLEEVE

GASTRIC SLEEVE BARIATRIC COOKBOOK

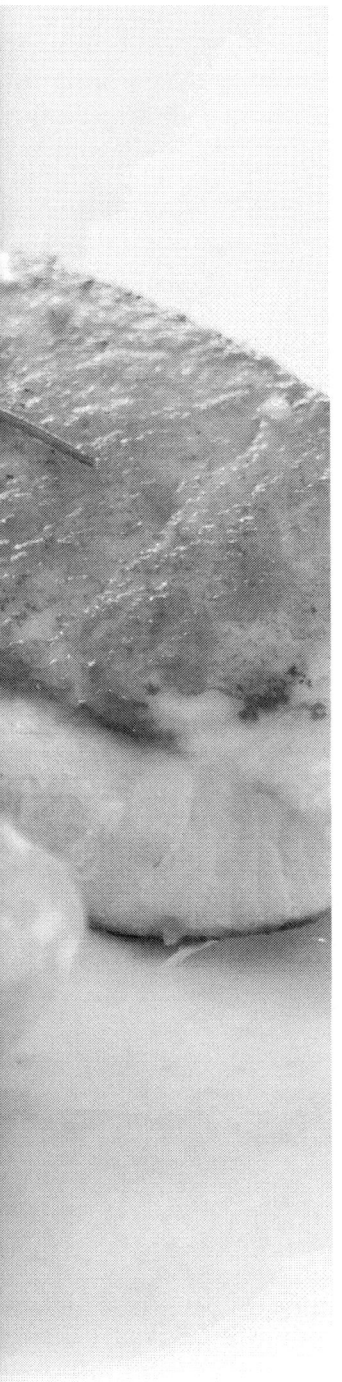

BENEFITS OF GASTRIC SLEEVE SURGERY

With gastric sleeve surgery, you go to reduce the size of the stomach by exporting part of it. This then leads to the reduction of the stomach and consequently to eating less because you feel full with less food, thus losing weight. Due also to the weight reduction, patients experience an overall improvement in health over time by reducing or completely eliminating medications.

WHAT TO EAT.

One of the most frequently asked questions for those who have had bariatric sleeve surgery is, "What can I eat now?" this chapter will walk you through how to prepare for surgery, and the best part is to be successful after surgery, including what to eat to heal and live with the sleeve.

BENEFITS

MINIMUM INVASION the surgery takes about 40 to 70 minutes and only small incisions are made.

PORTION CONTROL by decreasing the size of the stomach, automatically the patient will feel full with little food.

LESS HUNGER this type of operation causes the patient to feel less hungry because the part of the stomach that produces ghrelin, the hunger hormone, is removed.

MINIMUM RESTRICTIONS IN DIET this surgery allows for no major changes in diet. One just has to be careful not to eat foods with added fats and sugars.

HAVING SWEETS WITHOUT DUMPING SYNDROME dumping is a condition that happens to people who have had gastric bypass. After eating foods high in sugars or in some cases, high in carbohydrates, they may feel shaky, light-headed, sweat, or feel dizzy; may increase heart rate; have low blood sugar; abdominal cramps; diarrhea.

This usually doesn't happen to people who have had gastric sleeve, although still a large amount of sugar can cause a dumping syndrome.

MINDFUL EATING

Practicing mindful eating means eating without distractions this is the key to being able to eat the right foods and the right amount of food.

Avoid distractions. When you eat, sit comfortably and focus on what you are eating. Don't get distracted by TV, phone, etc.

Chew properly. Try to chew your food properly and don't talk while eating because you might ingest extra air and then feel uncomfortable.

Eat new things. One way not to be bored with what you eat is to try new things.

Paralyze your self-compassion. Silence your inner critic. Let go of every negative thought. When you realize you are having a negative thought say out loud "STOP" and replace it with a positive thought.

Practice positive affirmations. If you do something wrong, don't blame yourself; no one is perfect. And we do not seek perfection but we try to be better than the day before.

PART TWO

YOUR NEW LIFE

LIQUIDS

It is very important to stay hydrated after surgery for the first few months. Fluids are to be introduced slowly and 30 minutes before or after meals. You can drink water, decaf tea, sugar-free non-carbonated, low-sodium tomato or vegetable juice, sugar-free milk or milk alternative, salt-free broth, sugar-free hot chocolate, or popsicles.

Drink a minimum of 64 ounces per day of liquid.

Avoid: for the first few months avoid caffeine, sweetened fruit juices, soda, mint tea, and alcohol.

PROTEINS

Protein is the most important macronutrient in our diet and especially for those who have undergone gastric sleeve surgery. Protein is important for maintaining muscles, cellular and hormonal support, and our body. Since our bodies cannot build protein on their own, it's important to get enough from our food.

After surgery, you may need to supplement your diet with protein shakes or protein powder. When choosing protein prefers whey protein, choose those low in sugar and fat, and avoid hydrolyzed protein.

Avoid: High-fat foods such as cream, whole milk, fatty cuts of beef or pork, and skin on poultry.

PROTEIN	PORTION SIZE	PROTEIN (GR)
Beef, pork, poultry, fish	2 ounces	14 grams
Scallops, shrimp	3 onuces	18 grams
Turkey, ham, roast beef, chicken, or other lunch meat	2 ounces	10 grams
Eggs	1 large	6 grams
Egg whites	2 large	8 grams
Fat-free, 1% or 2% cottage or ricotta cheese	1/2 cup	14 grams
Cheddar, mozzarella, Swiss, and other natural cheese	1 ounce	7 grams
Non-fat Greek yogurt	6 ounces	15 grams
Lentils (cooked)	1/2 cup	9 grams
Beans (cooked)	1/2 cup	9 grams

CARBOHYDRATES

Carbohydrates are our primary source of energy. Avoiding carbohydrates completely can be the wrong way to go. In the long run, a diet high in protein and low in carbohydrates leads to a decrease in muscle mass. As our body needs energy, if we do not introduce carbohydrates it will go to use muscle mass as energy. Our liver also stores glycogen, which helps control blood sugar levels while we sleep. So we need to eat carbohydrates in order to help our liver store the sugar it needs.

Avoid: Refined grains, cookies, cakes, pastries, candies, fruit juice, and soda

CARBOHYDRATE	PORTION SIZE	CARBOHYDRATE (GR)
Fresh fruit	1/2 cup Reccomended 2-3 servings per day	5 grams
Vegetables	1 cup Recommended: 3-4 servings per day	7 grams
Oatmeal	1/2 cup	27 grams
Whole-grain bread	1 slice	15 grams
Brown rice	1/2 cup	16 grams
Whole-wheat pasta	1/3 cup	14 grams
Barley	1/3 cup	14 grams
Ancient grains (quinoa, millet, spelt, farro)	1/3 cup	13 grams

FATS

Fats are another very important macronutrient for our body. In fact, when we don't consume enough fat we can feel tired, hungry, and weak with little energy, and our skin can feel dry.

Limit: Butter, palm and coconut oil, and full-fat dairy.

Avoid: Animal fats, fried foods, margarine containing trans fats, and food high in saturated fats.

FAT	PORTION SIZE	FAT (GR)
Avocado	1 tablespoon	8 grams
Chia	2 tablespoons	7 grams
Olive oil	1 teaspoon	27 grams
Almonds	10 almonds	10 grams
Walnuts	2 tablespoons	8 grams
Peanuts	1/4 cup	14 grams
Nut butter	2 teaspoons	10 grams

VITAMINS

Supplements are very important for people who have had surgery. Always check with your doctor if you need supplements, but don't decide on your own whether to eliminate them from your diet.

It is very important to supplement vitamin D, B12, and calcium. Some patients also need vitamin B and iron.

FOODS TO AVOID

One of the biggest fears of people who have just had surgery is stomach pain or vomiting. The goal after this surgery is to have a normal life and go back to eating what you ate before the procedure. During the first 3 months after surgery, some foods should still be avoided to prevent precisely stomach pain or vomiting, but many foods can be added a little at a time allowing your body to adjust to your new stomach.

Liquids
Carbonated drinks
Alcohol
Caffeine
Fruit juice
Sugary beverages

Proteins
Breaded and deep-fried protein
Dry and tough meat

Carbs
Rice
Pasta
Bread
Dried fruits
Skin of fruit
Fresh pineapple

Pop corn
Granola and bran cereal

Fats
Raw nuts and seeds
Fried foods
Greasy foods
Nut butter

Other
Asparagus stalks
Raw celery
Coconut
Sweetened sauces or condiments
Cookies
Candy

KITCHEN TOOLS

To be successful on this journey you need to be able to get organized in time and have some tools to make your journey easier. Many of these you will already have in your kitchen, but in case you don't it would be better to get them, these also will help you cook in an easy and fun way.

Air fryer

Aluminum foil, nonstick Baking dishes (glass or ceramic)

Baking sheets and sheet pans

Blender

Cutting board

Food scale

Glass storage containers (varying sizes)

Measuring cups and spoons (for dry and liquid ingredients)

Mini food processor

Mixing bowls (small, medium, and large)

Muffin tins

Parchment paper

Plastic or silicone zip-top storage bags (varying sizes)

Plastic wrap

Pots and pans with lids (varying sizes)

Ramekins (6 ounces)

Sharp knife

Slow cooker

Spatula, whisk, tongs, mixing spoons

Spiralizer

Vegetable peeler

SHOPPING LIST

Here's a mini shopping list for when you first set up your bariatric kitchen.

- Almond flour
- Dried lentils
- Canned beans
- Dried spices and herbs
- Canned tuna, chicken, and salmon
- Eggs
- Olive oil
- Nuts and seeds
- Unsweetened pasta sauce
- Oats
- Whole wheat flour
- Low-sodium broth (vegetable, beef, and chicken)
- Frozen fruit
- Frozen vegetables
- Frozen meats
- Low- or no-fat dairy

If you still have food in your cupboard from your pre-VSG life, I suggest you donate anything that you can't use to a local food bank or a family in need.

Do a sweep of your kitchen, and if you see any of the following, clear it out.

- Boxed potatoes
- Bread
- Baked beans
- Cookies
- Chips
- Candy
- Cereal
- Crackers
- Frozen desserts
- Dried fruit
- High-carb frozen meals
- Sugary condiments
- High-fat products
- Refined pasta
- White rice
- Popcorn
- Caffeine

EATING AT A RESTAURANT

In the first few weeks after surgery, you will opt to eat at home and prepare your own food. Eating with friends and family is still an important part of your social life. I'll leave you with some tips so you can choose the healthiest option for when you go to a restaurant.

1. **Get organized.** Many restaurants have online menus. Take a look at it so you already know what to choose once you're at the restaurant.

2. **Ask for dressing on the side.** Whenever possible, choose dressings that are low in calories, fat, and sugar, such as balsamic vinegar, mustard, or salsa.

3. **Pay attention to certain words on the menu**, such as steamed, garden fresh, and broiled, which indicate healthier methods of cooking. Pay attention to the words cheesy, butter sauce, sautee, and breaded. They usually indicate foods high in calories.

4. **Check macronutrients.** Opt for high-protein choices such as chicken, fish, and shrimp, and choose a side of healthy carbohydrates such as quinoa, steamed vegetables, and corn.

5. **Order from the kid's menu.** In some restaurants, it is possible to order from the kid's menu. Usually, these portions are smaller and may also have the option of a healthier side dish such as fruit or steamed vegetables. If this is not possible, ask for a to-go box so you can set aside half the food that comes on your plate.

8 Weeks After Surgery

It is important to plan your meals in advance so you can get the right macronutrient intake and not skip meals. A simple and practical tip is to cook plenty so you can eat leftovers the next day or freeze them to eat later.
I hope you can follow the eight-week meal plan to make meal planning easier after surgery. But always follow the directions given by your surgery center.

WEEK 1 AND 2
LIQUID DIET.
The first two weeks are all about fluids. Having enough fluids leads to building the right foundation to be able to drink enough fluids over the long term. Here are some important factors to keep in mind.
A liquid diet means.
- Drinking at least 64 ounces of liquids.
- Be careful that the shakes have no seeds or pulp
- If you drink protein shakes for every meal, it would be a good idea to have high-protein milk for snacks.

WEEK 3
PUREE DIET.
The consistency of puree is thicker than liquid and at this point allows you to have a wider variety of food. Anything can be pureed as long as you have a good blender.
While you're at this stage first focus on hydration, then protein intake and finally supplement with fruits and vegetables.
Use Greek yogurt, broth, or water to achieve the desired consistency.
Use herbs and seasonings to add flavor to your dishes.

WEEK 4-5-6
SOFT DIET.
Soft food is defined as food that you can cut with a fork. Now that your stomach has gotten used to digesting food with more texture, you can introduce more different kinds of food and drink fewer protein shakes.
Portions may vary, but roughly you will be able to eat ½ cup of food.
Introduce one or two new varieties of food at a time, and remember to stay hydrated.

WEEK 7-8
Congratulations! You've done it! At this point, your stomach should be healed, and you will now be able to set the blender aside and have regular food. At this point, you can add new foods to your meals but be careful not to introduce several new foods at the same time. For the first few months, you can continue to drink protein shakes between meals to maintain adequate protein intake.

PART THREE

LIQUID FOOD

Banana Smoothie

Prep Time: 5 mins, Cook Time: 5 mins, Servings: 1

¼ cup nonfat Greek yogurt

1 cup banana, sliced (frozen is best)

¼ tsp vanilla extract

¼ cup low fat milk (almond, dairy, etc.)

1. In a blender, combine all the ingredients. Blend till completely smooth. Add extra low fat milk if necessary to get the desired consistency.
2. Serve right away.

Nutritions

Calories: 8 kcal, Carbohydrates: 39 g, Protein: 9 g, Fats: 3 g

Mango Smoothie

Prep Time: 5 mins, Cook Time: 5 mins, Servings: 10 oz.

¼ cup plain nonfat Greek yogurt

½ medium banana (frozen)

¾ cup low fat milk

¼ tsp vanilla extract

1 ½ cups frozen mango pieces

1. Take a blender, combine all of the ingredients. Blend until smooth. Add extra low fat milk as needed to thin down the smoothie. Serve right away.

Nutritions

Calories: 173 kcal, Carbohydrates: 31 g, Protein: 7 g, Fats: 4 g

Cocoa Almond Protein Smoothie

Prep Time: 5 mins, Cook Time: 5 mins, Servings: 1

¼ cup plus 2 tbsp of low fat milk (almond, dairy, etc.)
¾ cup nonfat Greek yogurt
1 medium banana (sliced and frozen)
2 tbsp almond butter
½ tbsp unsweetened cocoa powder
¾ cup ice cubes

1. In a blender and blend all recipe Ingredients. Mix till smooth.
2. Enjoy!

Nutritions

Calories: 471 kcal, Carbohydrates: 45 g, Protein: 27 g, Fats: 23 g

High-Protein Milk

Prep Time: 5 mins, Cook Time: 0 mins, Servings: 4

4 cups low-fat milk
1⅓ cups instant nonfat dry milk powder

1. In a large pitcher, mix the milk and milk powder well. 2. Chill in the refrigerator for up to 5 days.

Nutritions

Calories: 127, fat: 3g, protein: 11g, carbs: 15g, fiber: 0g, sugar: 13g

Apple and Peanut Butter Smoothie

1 serving, 5 min to prepare, and 5 min to cook

1 scoop of Protein Powder Vanilla
1 cup of unsweetened almond low fat milk
1 sliced apple
Sprinkle of nutmeg
1 tbsp Natural Peanut Butter
Cinnamon to taste

Blend together 1 tablespoon of natural peanut butter,

1 tablespoon of protein powder,

1 cup of low-fat almond milk, and 1 sliced apple.

Utilize a spice grinder to grind up some cinnamon and nutmeg.

Continue blending until the mixture becomes silky smooth.

Nutritions

Calories: 284 kcal, Carbohydrates: 22 g, Protein: 20 g, Fats: 12.5 g

Blueberry Coconut Water Smoothie

Prep Time: 15 mins, Cook Time: 0 mins, Servings: 1

1 ½ cups blueberries (frozen)

1 cup coconut water

½ cup Greek or full-fat plain yogurt

¼ tsp coconut extract

1. Blend all Ingredients well until smooth puree forms. Pour it in a glass and serve.

Nutritions

Calories: 301kcal, Carbohydrates: 49g, Protein: 17g , Fat: 5g

Savory Beef Bone Broth

Prep time: 5 minutes , Cook time: 5 to 8 hours, Makes 8 cups

Nonstick cooking spray
1 medium yellow onion, chopped
1 cup diced celery
1 cup peeled, diced carrot
3 pounds beef bones
1 pound stew beef
12 cups water
1 teaspoon salt
2 bay leaves
1 tablespoon minced garlic

1. Preheat the oven to 400°F (205°C). Coat a shallow roasting pan with cooking spray and set aside.
2. Arrange the onion, celery, and carrot in an even layer in the roasting pan. Place the beef bones and stew beef in the pan on top of the vegetables. Roast the bones, meat, and vegetables for 40 minutes, flipping the meat and bones halfway through the cooking time.
3. Remove the pan from the oven and place the bones, meat, and vegetables into a large stock pot. Add the water, salt, bay leaves, and garlic and bring to a rolling boil.
4. Reduce the heat to medium low and simmer for at least 4 hours. Supervise the pot during the simmering process, stirring a few times an hour.
5. Using a strainer spoon, remove the bones, meat, and vegetables from the pot. Enjoy the broth warm.
6. Store the leftover bone broth in an airtight container in the refrigerator for up to 3 days or freeze for up to 1 year.

Nutritions

Calories: 138kcal, Carbohydrates: 2g, Protein: 13g, Fat: 8g

Southwest-Style Chicken Bone Broth

Prep time: 5 minutes , Cook time: 5 to 8 hours, Makes 8 cups

Nonstick cooking spray

4 large carrots, peeled and chopped

1 medium red onion, quartered

1 large tomato, quartered

1 red bell pepper, sliced

1 (5- to 7-pound / 2.3- to 3.2-kg) whole chicken

12 to 16 cups water

1 teaspoon salt

1 teaspoon ground cumin

1 teaspoon dried cilantro

2 bay leaves

1. Preheat the oven to 400°F (205°C). Coat a shallow broiler pan with nonstick cooking spray.
2. Arrange the carrot, onion, tomato, and bell pepper in an even layer in the pan. Place the chicken in the pan and roast for 90 minutes or more (about 20 minutes per pound of chicken), until a thermometer inserted in the thigh reads 165°F (74°C) and the juices run clear.
3. Remove the pan from the oven and remove the meat from carcass, setting aside for other recipes.
4. Place the carcass and vegetables in a large pot. Add enough water to the pot to cover the carcass and vegetables completely. Add the salt, cumin, cilantro, and bay leaves to the pot and bring to a rolling boil.
5. Reduce the heat to medium and simmer for at least 4 hours, or longer for increased flavor. Supervise the pot during the simmering process, stirring a few times an hour.
6. Use a strainer spoon to remove the bones, meat, and vegetables from the pot. Enjoy the broth warm.
7. Store the leftover bone broth in an airtight container for up to 3 days or freeze for up to 1 year.

Nutritions

Calories: 138, fat: 2g, protein: 15g, carbs: 1g, fiber: 0g, sugar: 0g, sodium: 400mg

PART FOUR

PUREE FOOD

Pumpkin Pie Chia Pudding

Prep Time: 10 mins, Cook Time: 8 hrs 10 mins, Servings: 4

- 2 cups canned coconut low fat milk
- 1 cup puree pumpkin
- ¼ cup sugar coconut
- 1 tsp cinnamon
- ½ tsp ginger
- ½ tsp nutmeg
- ¼ tsp allspice
- ½ cup seeds chia

1. Add all the ingredients to a blender, except the chia seeds, and mix till smooth. Pulse till the chia seeds are blended.
2. Cover and chill the mix overnight in four mason jars.

Nutritions

Calories: 252 kcal, Carbohydrates: 24 g, Protein: 5 g, Fat: 16 g

Chocolate Rice Pudding

Prep Time: 5 mins, Cook Time: 30 mins, Servings: 5

- 2/3 cup rice brown
- 3 cups canned coconut low fat milk
- ½ cup maple syrup
- 1/8 tsp kosher salt or sea
- ½ tsp cinnamon
- ½ cup chocolate chips dark
- 1 tsp vanilla extract

1. Over high temperature, bring water & rice to your boil. Reduce the heat to a low setting & cover.
2. Cook the rice for approximately 15 mins, or till all the water has been absorbed.
3. Meanwhile, bring cinnamon, maple syrup, coconut low fat milk, & salt to your simmer in a different saucepan. Toss in the cooked rice. Reduce heat & simmer, occasionally stirring, for approximately 15 minutes, or until your pudding is fully thickened.
4. Remove from the heat and mix in vanilla extract. Serve warm, or chill for one hour before serving cold.

Nutritions

Calories: 325 kcal, Carbohydrates: 34 g, Protein: 3 g, Fat: 22 g

Caramel Apple Bread Pudding

Prep Time: 20 Mins, Cook Time: 30 Mins, Servings: 6

- 1 cup unsweetened applesauce
- 1 cup low fat milk almond
- ½ cup of maple syrup
- 3 large eggs
- 1 tsp extract vanilla
- 1 tsp cinnamon ground
- ¼ tsp nutmeg ground
- 5 cups bread whole-wheat
- 1 cup fresh, peeled apples

1. Pre-heat your oven to 325°F. Use nonstick spray to coat a casserole dish lightly.
2. Pour everything into a large mixing basin, but the bread and apple. Top the bread pieces with diced apples on the plate. Overlay the bread & apples with an applesauce mixture. Add extra liquid after 5 Mins of sitting. Once liquid & bread mix is ¼" from the top of your casserole dish, repeat this procedure until it is done.
3. The rack of your oven should be filled with water. Your bread pudding mixture should be placed on the rack above the water dish. 'Make sure a toothpick put into the middle comes out clean after 30-40 Mins of baking time. Golden brown is the perfect color for the top. Add extra water to the pan if it gets low. Serve at room temperature after allowing it to settle for around 10 Mins.

Nutritions

Calories: 199 kcal, Carbohydrates: 37 g, Protein: 7 g, Fat: 3 g

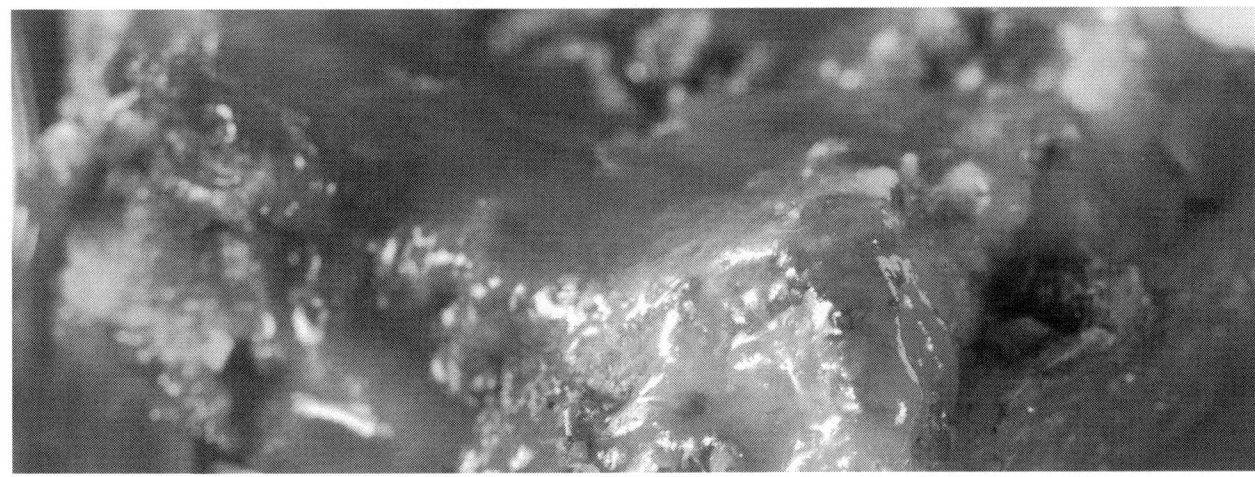

Coconut Low-Fat Milk Tapioca Pudding

Prep Time: 2 Mins, Cook Time: 25 Mins, Servings: 3

1/3 cup tapioca pearls small

1 cup low fat milk almond

13 oz unsweetened canned coconut low fat milk

¼ cup maple syrup

1 tsp extract vanilla

1 salt pinch

1 cut & cubed mango

½ cup rinsed & dried raspberries

1. For at least one hours, soak the tapioca pearls into almond low fat milk.

2. Add the almond low-fat milk-tapioca pearl and the coconut low fat milk to a saucepan. Immediately after bringing the mixture to a boil, reduce the heat to a simmer and whisk regularly to avoid scorching the pearls.

3. Simmer the mix for twenty minutes, stirring every few Mins. Ensure the pudding simmer at a moderate and steady temperature to avoid overcooking.

4. Add the vanilla, maple syrup, & salt just before serving. Take the pan off the heat and continue to stir for an additional 1-2 Mins.

5. Traditional tapioca pudding is served chilled. If you've tiny ramekins or plates, divide the mixture into them. The ideal cool time is 2 hrs. Before eating heated pudding, allow it to cool for almost ten mins in the serving dish.

6. 3 mango cubes & 2-3 raspberries on each ramekin should be enough to fill a quarter cup.

Nutritions

Calories: 181 kcal, Carbohydrates: 15 g, Protein: 2 g, Fat: 14g

Crustless Vegetable Quiche

Prep Time: 15 mins, Cook Time: 30 mins, Servings: 2

- 1 tbsp olive oil
- 2 small diced yellow onion
- 2 minced garlic cloves
- ½ cup pepper diced red bell
- ½ cup bell pepper diced
- ½ cup sliced zucchini
- 6 florets broccoli
- ¼ cup tomatoes diced sun-dried
- 3 large eggs
- 4 large egg whites
- 2 tbsp low-fat low fat milk
- 1 tsp oregano dried
- ½ tsp pepper black
- sea salt

1. The oven should be preheated at 425 F.
2. Sauté onion & garlic in oil within a large pan over moderate heat for 4 mins or until soft. Toss in the vegetables & continue to cook for another 2 mins before adding the sun-dried tomatoes.
3. Mix the eggs, low fat milk, egg whites, seasonings & in a small mixing bowl. Toss the sautéed veggies into a 9" pie plate sprayed with cooking spray. Cover all of the vegetables with the egg mixture.
4. Preheat the oven to 425°F for 10 min; then, drop the temperature to 350°F & bake for another 20-25 mins. Once the quiche puffs & a knife put in the middle come out clear, it's done baking.

Nutritions
Calories: 141 kcal, Carbohydrates: 15 g, Protein: 11 g, Fat: 5 g

Mint Chocolate Protein Pots de Creme

Prep time: 5 mins, Cook time: 20 mins, Servings: 4

1 cup of low fat milk (your choice)

2 servings of chocolate protein powder (your favorite one)

1/8 tsp of mint extract

2 tbsp cocoa powder, unsweetened

2 tbsp maple syrup

½ tsp of vanilla extract

2 eggs, large

1. Preheat the oven to 325 F. Set a kettle or saucepan of water to boil as well.
2. In the blender, mix the low-fat milk, cocoa powder, protein, vanilla extract & maple syrup until smooth (about 16-20 secs). Add the eggs.
3. In the baking dish, place 4 ramekins and divide the mixture equally. Put the baking tray on the center rack in the oven that has been preheated.
4. Fill the baking tray halfway with hot water.
5. Bake for 18-20 mins but check on it after 10 mins. The top may immediately produce a brownie-like crust. They might still be a bit dangly when you jiggle the ramekins, but the interior must not be watery. It's not a huge deal if you cook them far beyond the exact point when they're jiggly. The finished texture is more fudge-like than custard-like.

Nutritions

Calories: 90 kcal, Carbohydrates: 10 g, Protein: 10.1 g, Fats: 4 g

Creamy Shrimp Scampi Puree

Prep Time: 8 Mins, Cook Time: 0 Mins, Servings: 8

1 lb Shrimp
4 Cloves garlic, minced
2 tbsp Olive oil
2 tbsp Low fat plain nonfat Greek yogurt
¼ cup Parsley, chopped

1. Heat some olive oil in a large pan over medium-high heat.
2. Dry the shrimp and place them in the heated pan. Cook, tossing halfway through, for 2-3 mins, or until barely pink. Cook for another min, or until garlic is aromatic.
3. Transfer to a heat-resistant bowl. Toss in the Greek yogurt and parsley to coat.
4. Fill a food processor halfway with the mix and pulse until smooth.

Nutritions

Calories: 91.8 kcal, Carbohydrates: 0.9 g, Protein: 14.1 g, Fats: 3.7 g

Banana Peanut Butter Protein "Minute Pudding"

Prep time: 5 mins, Cook time: 0 mins, Servings: 2-4

½ cup cottage cheese
1 scoop protein powder
2 tbsp. powdered peanuts
1 tsp maple syrup

1. Add the Banana and peanut powder, maple syrup, and cheese to a blender and process for 5 mins.
2. Pour into the glasses and enjoy your pudding.

Nutritions

Calories: 98 kcal, Carbohydrates: 5 g, Protein: 10 g, Fat: 3 g

Scan the QR code to instantly access the vibrant Cookbook and Journal. Your culinary adventure and health insights await!

PART FIVE

SOFT FOOD

Low-Carb Pancakes

Prep time: 10 mins, Cook time: 15 mins, Servings: 4

- 1 pkg+ 1 extra tsp. Protein Baking Mix
- 1 tbsp. banana pudding mix, sugar-free
- 2 tbsp. unflavored nonfat Greek yogurt
- 3 tbsp. low fat milk
- 1 beaten egg
- ¼ tsp. pure vanilla extract

For topping:

- low-calorie butter spray
- ¼ banana, sliced
- ¼ cup sugar-free pancake syrup
- 1/8 tsp. rum extract
- 1/8 tsp. cinnamon

1. Coat a grill pan with non-stick butter spray and place it on medium heat to heat up.
2. Meanwhile, in a mixing bowl, thoroughly combine all ingredients. If the batter is too thick, add a tablespoon of low fat milk at a time until it approaches the consistency of a pudding.
3. Drop piles of the mixture on a pan with a spoon and spread them out into circles. Cook each side for 1-2 mins on one side. When done, transfer to a plate.
4. To create the topping, place a small pan (7 1/8 inch) on medium heat and coat it with non - stick cooking spray. Spray the bananas with butter spray and cook for a few mins. Add the pancake syrup and allow to boil before lowering the heat. Stir in the rum essence and cinnamon, then serve on top of the pancakes.

Nutritions

Calories: 480 kcal, Carbohydrates: 24g, Proteins: 23 g, Fat: 0g

Souffle Omelets with Mushrooms

Prep Time: 10 Mins, Cook Time: 15 Mins, Servings: 1

- 1 tsp oil olive
- 1 minced clove garlic
- 8 oz sliced mushrooms
- 1 tbsp minced parsley
- 3 separated large eggs
- ¼ cup of cheddar cheese shredded fat-free

1. In a pan, heat olive oil on medium heat & cook the garlic.
2. Sauté your mushrooms for ten Mins. Remove from heat and add the parsley.
3. In a bowl, beat your egg yolks till they are pale yellow and thick. To begin with, whip the egg whites until they're foamy white. Add salt, cheese, & pepper to the yolks before folding within whites.
4. Use nonstick spray to coat a big skillet. Cover and let the egg mix sit for a few Mins. In other words, don't stop cooking until you have a golden-brown crust on the top & bottom. To make an omelet, add mushrooms and then fold the omelet over.

Nutritions

Calories: 329 kcal, Carbohydrates: 10 g, Protein: 31 g, Fat: 19g

Strawberry Chia Overnight Oats

Prep Time: 5 Mins, Cook Time: 5 Mins, Servings: 4

½ cup low fat milk
¼ cup Greek yogurt
½ cup old fashioned oats
¼ tsp vanilla extract
½ cup old fashioned oats
¼ cup sliced strawberries
1 ½ tsp chia seeds

1. In a glass jar or dish, combine all items except the strawberries. To mix, cover securely with a lid, then shake vigorously (or stir).
2. Refrigerate for at least one night.
3. Before serving, mix in the strawberries and serve. Overnight oats are usually eaten cold, although they may be warmed in your microwave if needed.

Nutritions

Calories: 286 kcal, Carbohydrates: 45 g, Protein: 16 g, Fats: 5 g

Tuna Salad

Prep Time: 10 Mins, Cook Time: 10 Mins, Servings: 1

½ cup low fat milk
¼ cup Greek yogurt
½ cup old fashioned oats
¼ tsp vanilla extract
½ cup old fashioned oats
¼ cup sliced strawberries
1 ½ tsp chia seeds

1. Take a medium dish, place the drained tuna.
2. Combine the Greek yogurt, relish, celery, red onion, and a pinch of salt and pepper in a mixing bowl.
3. Stir everything together using a fork till completely blended. Taste and season with extra pepper and salt, if necessary.
4. Serve the tuna salad over a bed of lettuce in avocado halves or hallow tomatoes for a low-carb option.

Nutritions

Calories: 78 kcal, Carbohydrates: 3 g, Protein: 15 g, Fats: 2 g

Protein Pumpkin Cheesecake Cups

Prep time: 10 mins, Cook time: 10 mins, Servings: 4

1/2 cup of canned pumpkin (not pumpkin pie filling!)

1 serving of Protein powder

8 oz cream cheese softened, low fat

2 tbsp of Greek yogurt vanilla, low fat

1/2 tsp of pumpkin pie spice

Topping

½ cup of crushed cereal

2 tbsp of walnut pieces

1. Mix pumpkin & protein powder in a dish. With the help of a hand mixer, beat on medium speed until completely mixed.
2. Beat cream cheese, pie spice & Greek yogurt for 1-2 mins on medium speed, then for 1-2 mins on high speed, or till smooth.
3. Place a half-cup portion in each of 4 cups.
4. Combine nuts & cereal in a blender & pour equal quantities of topping into each cup. To serve, garnish with a pinch of cinnamon.

Nutritions

Calories: 130, Carbohydrates: 17 g, Protein: 14 g, Fats: 6.6 g

Strawberry & Honey Banana Soft Serve

Prep Time: 5 mins, Cook Time: 0 mins, Servings: 3 cups

2 ½ cups frozen sliced banana

1 ½ cups frozen sliced strawberry

1 cup Honey Almond Low fat milk

1. Chop the frozen fruits several times in a blender until it is coarsely chopped.
2. Reduce the speed and gradually pour the almond low fat milk until it is well absorbed and creamy.
3. Serve right away or store in tiny portions in the freezer to take out and enjoy later.

Nutritions

Calories: 427kcal, Carbohydrates: 85g, Protein: 9g, Fat: 10 g

Blueberry French Toast Casserole

Prep Time: 15 mins, Cook Time: 30 mins, Servings: 3

- 2 cups bread whole-grain
- 4 large egg whites
- 1 cup of low fat milk coconut
- 2 tbsp maple syrup
- 1 tsp extract vanilla
- ½ tsp extract almond
- 1 tsp cinnamon ground
- 1 cup fresh blueberries

1. Preheated at 350°F and spray a casserole dish with a non-stick spray. Set aside your sliced bread within the dish that has been made.
2. Mix well all the other ingredients, but the blueberries, in a plate. Cut the bread in cube, mix it with the blueberries and pour the mix over the bread.
3. Bake for around 30-40 mins, or unless the casserole is gently browned & bread cubes have absorbed all of the liquid from the casserole.

Nutritions

Calories: 123 kcal, Carbohydrates: 13 g, Protein: 4 g, Fat: 7 g

PART SIX

BREAKFAST

Protein Pancakes

Prep Time: 5 mins, Cook Time: 5 Mins, Servings: 1

- 1 tbsp maple syrup
- ½ cup Protein Pancake Mix
- ¼ cup sliced almonds

1. Prepare pancakes and drizzle with 1 tbsp of maple syrup.
2. Sprinkle sliced almonds over them.

Nutritions

Calories: 360 kcal, Carbohydrates: 42 g, Protein: 21 g, Fats: 12.5 g

Butternut Squash Breakfast Wraps

Prep Time: 20 Mins, Cook Time: 25 Mins, Servings: 6

- 4 cups diced butternut squash
- ½ cup wilted Spinach
- 16 low fat Turkey Sausage Links, cooked
- 1 cup low fat Cheddar Cheese, Shredded
- 6 Eggs
- 6 Whole Wheat High Fiber Tortillas
- Salt and Pepper
- 3 Tbsp Butter
- ¼ cup Low fat milk

1. Melt half butter portion in a pan over medium flame.
2. Sprinkle pepper and salt over a diced butternut squash.
3. When the butter is simmering add half squash and cook until it gets brown. Toss in the pan and continue to cook until golden brown on both sides and squash becomes tender.
4. Set aside on a plate and continue to sauté the remaining squash.
5. Cook the turkey sausages till they are thoroughly done. Cut into tiny pieces and set aside on a plate.
6. Wilt the spinach in a pan until it is completely wilted.
7. Whisk the low fat milk, eggs, salt, and pepper in the mixing bowl.
8. In a pan, melt the remaining butter and bring to a simmer. Cook the eggs until they are scrambled.
9. To assemble, cheddar cheese, eggs, spinach, squash, and sausage on each tortilla wrap. Let's wrap things up.

Nutritions

Calories: 109.5 kcal, Carbohydrates: 9.5 g, Protein: 9.5 g, Fats: 3.9 g

Chia Overnight Spiced Oats

Prep Time: 5 Mins, Cook Time: 45 Mins, Servings: 4

- 3 cups rolled oats old fashioned
- 3 tbsp maple syrup
- 2 tbsp chia seeds
- 2 ½ cups almond low fat milk, unsweetened
- 2-3 tsp chai spice homemade mix
- Toppings: dried fruit sliced almonds

1. Take a medium mixing bowl to combine the chia seeds, oats, spices, and maple syrup. Stir in the almond low fat milk until it is well incorporated. Refrigerate overnight.
2. Enjoy the breakfast.

Nutritions

Calories: 157 kcal, Carbohydrates: 26 g, Protein: 5 g, Fats: 4 g

Blueberry Baked Oatmeal Cups

Prep Time: 10 Mins, Cook Time: 25 Mins, Servings: 12

- 3 cups old-fashioned rolled oats
- 1 tsp of ground cinnamon
- 1 cup low fat milk
- 1 tsp of baking powder
- ¼ tsp salt
- ¼ cup honey
- 2 tbsp maple syrup
- 1 tsp extract vanilla
- 2 eggs large 1
- 1 cup fresh blueberries

1. Preheat your oven to 350 Fahrenheit. Set aside a (12-count) muffin tray that has been sprayed with cooking spray (nonstick).
2. Take a large mixing bowl, whisk together the baking powder, oats, salt, and cinnamon.
3. Whisk together the eggs, low fat milk, honey, vanilla extract, and brown sugar in a separate bowl until well blended. Combine the wet and dry ingredients in a mixing bowl and stir until thoroughly combined.
4. Use a big spoon, evenly spread the mixture among the muffin pan's 12 holes. Make sure all cups have an equal quantity of oats and liquid. Using your fingers, carefully press the blueberries into all oatmeal cups.
5. Bake for 25-27 mins at 350°F, or until the oatmeal cups' tops is hard. Remove from oven and let it cool for about 5-10 mins in the pan.
6. Remove all oatmeal cups and cool completely on a wire rack.

Nutritions

Calories: 126 kcal, Carbohydrates: 23 g, Protein: 3.7 g, Fats: 2.6 g

Fruit on The Bottom Yogurt

Prep Time: 5 Mins, Cook Time: 5 Mins, Servings: 4

4 cups plain nonfat Greek

3 cups blueberries

4 tbsp. unsalted butter

¼ cup sliced almonds, toasted

1 tbsp cornstarch

4 fresh raspberries

Nutritions

Calories: 157 kcal, Carbohydrates: 26 g, Protein: 5 g, Fats: 4 g

1. Take a mixing bowl to combine the yogurt and 1 ½ tsp of honey. Blend well until everything is well combined. Refrigerate it.
2. Heat the blueberries, 3 tbsp of honey, and 2 tsp water in a small skillet over medium-low heat.
3. Combine the 1 tsp cold water and cornstarch in a small mixing dish and stir until completely dissolved.
4. When the blueberries simmer, they'll eventually break down.
5. Add the cornstarch and continue to cook until the corn starch mixture thickens, then remove from the heat.
6. Refrigerate until cold and solidify, then transfer to containers.
7. Pour the yogurt over the fruit that has been allowed to cool.
8. Serve with almonds and raspberries.

Perfect Steel Cut Oats

Prep Time: 5 Mins, Cook Time: 25 Mins, Servings: 3

1 cup steel-cut oats

1 cup almond low fat milk

3 cups water

1/8 tsp salt

¼ tsp cinnamon

½ tsp vanilla extract

1 tsp pure maple syrup

Nutritions

Calories: 169 kcal, Carbohydrates: 27 g, Protein: 6 g, Fats: 3 g

1. Combine the low fat milk and water. Over medium-high heat, bring to a boil.
2. Reduce the heat and add salt and oats to the pan.
3. Cook, often stirring, for 20-30 mins or till the oats reach your preferred texture. Cook for about 20-25 mins if you want chewier oats; cook longer if you wish to soften oats, adding extra liquid as required.
4. Remove the pan and mix in the cinnamon, maple syrup, and vanilla extract.
5. As desired, add toppings.

Healthy Freezer Breakfast Burritos

Prep Time: 20 mins, Cook Time: 2 mins, Servings: 8 burritos

1 lb sausage (breakfast)

1/2 finely diced yellow onion

1/2 cored and diced red pepper

12 eggs

8 burrito-sized tortillas

2 cup low fat shredded cheddar cheese

1 cup chopped spinach

1. Cook the sausage in a heated pan for 2 mins until it is browned and crumbled. Set aside in a plate.
2. Add the chopped onions and bell pepper to the skillet and stir for 3 to 5 mins until softened. Meanwhile, gently whisk the eggs in a large mixing dish.
3. Turn the heat down to medium and scramble the eggs until fully cooked.
4. Turn the heat and let the egg scramble mixture cool fully.
5. Fill a tortilla with the prepared filling. Drizzle 1/4 cup of cheese on top, then firmly roll. Place it in the baking sheet and repeats the process until all of the burritos are done.
6. Freeze the baking sheet for about 1 min, or until solidly frozen, then move the burritos to the sealed bag or wrap each burrito separately in plastic wrap.
7. To reheat the tortilla, remove it from the plastic wrap and cover it loosely in a paper towel. Microwave each side for 45 secs on high.

Nutritions

Calories: 365kcal, Carbohydrates: 40g, Protein: 21g, Fat: 12g

Easy breakfast roll-ups

Prep Time: 15 Mins, Cook Time: 35 Mins, Servings: 6

1 egg

Salt and pepper

1 tsp water or low fat milk

1 soft taco size flour all-wheat tortilla

Fillings: baby spinach, avocado, turkey bacon, tomatoes, low fat cheese, crumbled sausage

1. Whisk the low fat milk/water and egg until smooth in a small mixing bowl. If desired, place the tortilla on a plate and add cheese topping.
2. Spray a pan equal to the size of a tortilla with cooking spray. Preheat a pan at the medium-low flame and pour the egg mixture into it. Cook till the egg is fully cooked and the liquid has evaporated. Add pepper and salt to taste.
3. Slide the fried egg immediately on top of the tortilla/cheese.
4. Optional fillings may be placed on top of the egg.
5. Roll up the tortilla tightly without ripping it or displacing the fillings. Serve by cutting it in half.

Nutritions

Calories: 150 kcal, Carbohydrates 13 g, Protein 8.6g, Fats 7.3 g

Turkey, Cheese, and Veggie Frittatas

Prep Time: 20 Mins, Cook Time: 20 Mins, Servings: 4

½ cup minced onion

2 tsp olive oil

1 ½ cups baby spinach

½ cup chopped bell pepper

¾ cup chopped cooked turkey

1 cup cooked quinoa

¾ cup grated low fat cheddar

7 eggs

½ cup unsweetened low fat milk

1/8 tsp pepper

½ tsp salt

1. Preheat your oven up to 350 degrees. Grease a muffin tray with cooking spray.
2. Take a medium pan and heat the olive oil over medium heat. Cook, stirring periodically, for 3-5 mins, or until the bell pepper and onion are softened. Cook them for about 30 sec or until the spinach is slightly wilted. Place the veggies in a large mixing bowl.
3. Add the cheddar cheese, turkey, and cooked quinoa to the bowl containing veggies.
4. Mix the low fat milk and eggs in a measuring cup. Combine the pepper and salt in a mixing bowl.
5. In the prepared muffin tray, divide the mixture equally among the 12 wells.
6. Bake for about 18 to 22 mins, or until set. Allow cooling for 3 mins in the pan. Remove each frittata from the pan. Serve.

Nutritions

Calories 214kcal, Carbohydrates 9 g, Protein 15 g, Fats 13g

PART SEVEN

SOUPS & STEWS

Bean and Lentil Soup

Prep Time: 10 Mins, Cook Time: 35 Mins, Servings: 2

- 2 garlic cloves (minced)
- 1 tbsp olive oil
- 2 carrots, peeled and diced small
- 1 yellow onion
- 1 cup dried lentils
- 15 oz of diced tomatoes can
- 1 tsp chili powder
- 15 oz black beans can (drained)
- ½ tsp black pepper
- ½ tsp cumin
- ½ tsp kosher salt
- 4 cups vegetable broth
- ½ tsp red pepper, crushed

1. Add olive oil to a big saucepan and fry the garlic for 1 min. Continue to sauté the carrots and onions until the onion is soft, about 5 mins.
2. Cover and mix all remaining ingredients.
3. Boil at medium heat, then lower to low heat and cook for 25-30 mins, or until carrots and lentils are cooked.

Nutritions

Calories: 171 kcal, Carbohydrates: 29 g, Protein: 10 g, Fats: 2 g

Tuscan White Bean Soup

Prep Time: 10-15 mins, Cook Time: 20 mins, Servings: 2

2 tbsp olive oil
2 medium and chopped sweet potatoes
1 medium onion
4 celery ribs
3 cloves garlic
½ tsp dried rosemary
½ tsp dried thyme
½ tsp salt
1/8 tsp black pepper
2 cans drained cannellini beans
4 cups low-sodium vegetable broth
1 medium chopped bunch kale without tough stems

1. In a large saucepan/Dutch oven, add the onion, celery, and sweet potatoes in heated olive oil and cook for 5 mins over medium heat.
2. Stir in the garlic, salt, pepper, rosemary, and thyme and cook for 30 secs. Add the beans and stock in a saucepan.
3. Turn the flame to high and bring the mixture to a boil. Cook for another 10 min with a closed lid, or until potatoes are cooked.
4. Toss the chopped kale and cook for 2 mins until the kale has wilted. Serve.

Nutritions

Calories 221kcal, Carbohydrates 39g, Protein 11g, Fat 5g

Sausage Kale Soup

Prep Time: 10 Mins, Cook Time: 45 Mins, Servings: 3

1 tbsp oil olive
1 diced yellow onion
2 diced carrots
2 diced celery stalks
3 minced garlic cloves
1 lb low fat turkey sausage
28 oz diced, canned tomatoes
1 tbsp Italian seasoning
6 cups low sodium chicken broth
2 tsp chili flakes red
15 oz drained & rinsed cannellini beans
1 lb kale roughly chopped, stem removed

1. Over moderate flame, in a large pot sauté the onion. When is golden add the sausage crumbles until crisp-tender.
2. Add the garlic, celery, carrots and seasoning and cook until the vegetable are soft.
3. Pour the canned tomatoes, the broth, the cannellini beans, and the chili flakes. Let it simmer for 15 minutes.
4. Stir in the kale and simmer until is wilted. Serve warm.

Nutritions

Calories 221kcal, Carbohydrates 39g, Protein 11g, Fat 5g

Homemade Roasted Tomato Soup

Prep Time: 15 mins, Cook Time: 1 hour and 10 mins, Servings: 6

1.5 pound Roma tomatoes
5 garlic cloves
2 tbsp olive oil
½ tsp salt kosher
¼ tsp black pepper
1 onions thinly sliced
2 cups vegetable broth
¼ cup fresh basil
¼ cup dried oregano

Nutritions

Calories 217 kcal, Carbohydrates 25 g, Protein: 3 g, Fat: 4 g

1. Preheat the oven to 400°F. Spread chopped tomatoes and garlic cloves on the baking sheet that has been lined with parchment paper. Add salt, & pepper to taste. Drizzle with olive oil. Roast for approximately 40-45 mins, or unless your tomatoes start burning, depending on the size of the tomatoes.
2. Meanwhile add ½ tbsp olive oil in a large pot and place over medium heat. Add the onion and stir them to coat with the oil. Usually take 20 min to caramelized the onions.
3. When the tomatoes and garlic are done roasting, cool them for 10 min and add them to a blender and blend until smooth. Add caramelized onion and basil and blend again.
4. Transfer everything in a big pot, turn on a medium low heat add oregano, broth and salt and pepper to taste. Simmer for 10 min.

Carrot Soup with Pumpkin Seeds

Prep Time: 5 mins, Cook Time: 25 mins, Servings: 3

5 cups broth vegetable
2 cups cooked & mashed carrots
½ cup puree pumpkin
1 tsp cumin ground
½ tsp coriander ground
¼ tsp pepper cayenne
½ tsp salt kosher
½ tsp cinnamon ground
½ tsp turmeric ground
½ cup plain nonfat Greek yogurt
¼ cup toasted & shells removed pumpkin seeds
2 tbsp olive oil extra virgin

1. In a big soup pot, combine the broth, carrots, pumpkin puree, salt, cinnamon, cayenne, cumin, coriander, & turmeric using a hand blender or food processor. Stirring regularly, bringing the soup to your boil, then lowering the heat to a simmer.
2. Simmer for another 20 mins or more, stirring often.
3. Top the soup with pumpkin seeds, yogurt, & olive oil before serving.

Nutritions

Calories 217 kcal, Carbohydrates 25 g, Protein: 3 g, Fat: 4 g

Turkey Sweet Potato Stew

Prep Time: 10 mins, Cook Time: 1 hr 15 mins, Servings: 6

2 tbsp olive oil extra virgin
1 diced small yellow onion
1 diced small green pepper
3 minced garlic cloves
1 peeled & diced carrot large
2 peeled & diced sweet potatoes
3 cups of boneless & skinless cooked & shredded turkey breast
28 oz tomatoes diced
1 tbsp paprika smoked
1 tsp oregano dried
1 tsp coriander ground
¼ tsp crushed pepper flakes red
6 cups low-sodium chicken broth
¼ cup plain nonfat Greek yogurt
2 tbsp chopped cilantro fresh

1. Heat the oil to medium-high heat in a wide soup pot. Mix in the carrots and onions. Cook unless the onions become translucent, but the carrots remain firm.
2. Add all other ingredients, excluding yogurt & cilantro. Stir often while the mixture comes to your boil.
3. Simmer for approximately an hour after bringing to a boil.
4. Top with both yogurt & cilantro before serving.

Nutritions

Calories 217 kcal, Carbohydrates 25 g, Protein: 3 g, Fat: 4 g

Sausage Quinoa & Roasted Veggie Soup

Prep time: 10 mins, Cook time: 25 mins, Servings: 2

1 medium chopped onion
1 large clove minced garlic
1 pkg. low-fat diced turkey smoked sausage
4 cups washed and chopped Swiss chard
1 + 3 cup water
2 cored tomatoes
4 cups roasted veggies
1 cup uncooked quinoa
Salt and pepper
1 tsp Herbs de Provence

Nutritions

Calories: 250 kcal, Carbohydrates: 18 g, Protein: 22 g, Fat: 3g

1. Coat a big saucepan with non-stick cooking spray and set it on medium heat. Mix in the onions and sauté until browned, then add the garlic and cook for a few mins until fragrant.
2. Toss in the sausage and cook until the sausage is browned. Add 1 cup of water and the Swiss chard. Allow the liquid to boil, scraping bottom of pot to loosen browned bits.
3. Add the tomatoes and cover for 5 mins. Remove the cover and the peel from the tomatoes. Mash them with a potato masher.
4. Add 3 more cups of water, roasted vegetables, and quinoa. Stir everything together well.
5. Cook for approximately 25 mins, or until the chard has wilted and the quinoa has thoroughly cooked. Take it off from the heat and leave it covered for another 10 mins before eating.

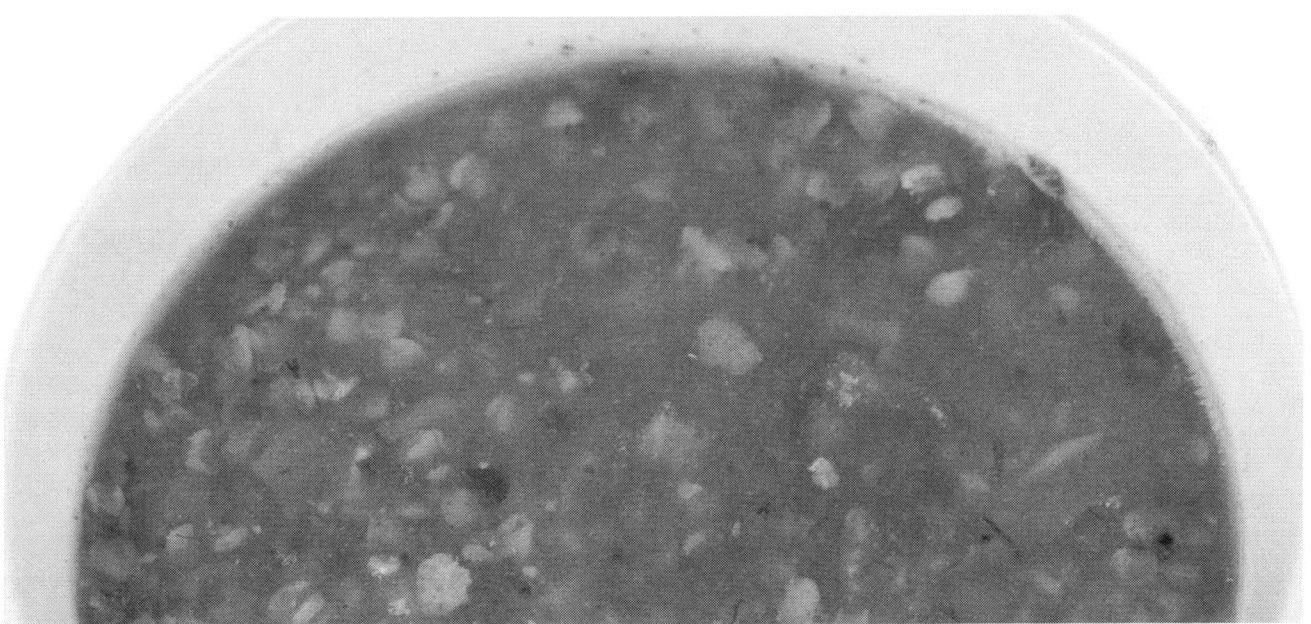

Peanut Stew

Prep time: 15 mins, Cook time: 40 mins, Servings: 4

1 tbsp of olive oil
1 small diced yellow onion
3 diced tomatoes
2 minced cloves of garlic
1 can or 12-15 ounces of peas & carrots
½ tsp of ground cumin
½ tsp of turmeric
½ tsp of ground coriander
1 tsp of garam masala
2 cups of water
1 cup of creamy peanut butter
4 ounces of tomato paste
¼ cup of sriracha sauce
3 cans or 15 ounces of garbanzo beans
4 cups of baby spinach
Salt & pepper, to taste

1. Preheat the soup pot on medium flame until it is hot. Toss in the garlic, olive oil & tomatoes. Cook for 2-3 mins.
2. Stir in the carrots & peas and all the water & spices and reduce the flame to low. Allow the liquid to come to a boil while covered.
3. In the mixing bowl, blend peanut butter and tomato paste till fully incorporated. Before putting everything again into the saucepan, spoon part of the vegetable mix into the dish & use it to thin it out.
4. Add the spicy sauce and stir thoroughly.
5. Stir in the baby spinach & garbanzo beans at the end. Cover the saucepan and cook for 26-30 mins on medium heat.

Nutritions

Calories: 107 kcal, Carbohydrates: 10.4 g, Protein: 14.4 g, Fats: 8 g

Cabbage Garlic Veggie Soup

Prep Time: 10 Mins, Cook Time: 30 Mins, Servings: 4

1 tbsp. extra-virgin olive oil
1 small chopped onion
1 chopped carrots,
1 stalks celery, minced
Kosher salt
Freshly ground black pepper
1 can white beans, drained and rinsed
1 cloves garlic, minced
1 tsp. thyme leaves
3 cup low-sodium chicken (or vegetable) broth
1 cup water
½ large head cabbage, chopped
1 can chopped fire-roasted tomatoes
1 tbsp. freshly chopped parsley

1. In a large pot heat olive oil on medium heat. Add the onions, celery, & carrots. Stirring constantly, cook for 5 mins until vegetables are soft.
2. Add garlic, beans and thyme and cook for about 30 sec.
3. Mix in tomatoes and cabbage and simmer for about 5 minute or until the cabbage is wilted.
4. Stir in parsley, remove immediately from heat and enjoy.

Nutritions

Calories: 74 kcal, Carbohydrates: 15 g, Protein: 3 g, Fat: 1g

PART EIGHT

VEGETABLES & SIDES

Balsamic-Glazed Roasted Acorn Squash with Cranberries and Goat Cheese

Prep Time: 10 Mins, Cook Time: 25 Mins, Servings: 2

1 acorn squash (~3 lb)
½ tsp dried rosemary
⅓ cup dried cranberries
1½ to 2 oz goat cheese, crumbled
½ cup balsamic vinegar
¼ tsp black pepper
1½ tbsp olive oil
⅛ tsp salt

1. Preheat your oven to around 375F. Meanwhile, microwave the acorn squash for 4 mins to make it easier to chop. Remove the bottom and top. After cutting in half (lengthwise), chop into 12-3/4-inch pieces. Use a parchment sheet or foil and line the baking sheet.
2. Place the squash slices on a plate. Season with rosemary, salt, and pepper. Drizzle the olive oil. Bake for 20-25 mins, or until vegetables are soft.
3. Allow the squash to cool after it has been removed from the oven. Drizzle with balsamic glaze, dried cranberries, and crumbled goat cheese.

Nutritions

Calories: 252 kcal, Carbohydrates: 56 g, Protein: 16 g, Fats: 8 g

Tuscan Salad Recipe with Mixed Greens and Lemon Caper Vinaigrette

Prep Time: 15 mins, Cook Time: 0 mins, Servings: 2

For Salad
1 cup chopped romaine lettuce
1 cup arugula baby
1 cup of radicchio
2 cup spinach baby
½ cup fat-free provolone cheese
¼ cup of capers
4 peeled & sliced eggs boiled
½ cup roughly chopped salmon cooked

For Dressing
1 & ½ tbsp juice lemon
1 tsp honey
1 tsp mustard Dijon
2 tbsp olive oil
½ tbsp capers

1. **For Salad** In a medium bowl, add all of the ingredients & gently mix.
2. **For Dressing** Use a blender to mix all the dressing ingredients, drizzle it over the top and enjoyed!

Nutritions

Calories 377 kcal, Carbohydrates 6 g, Protein 25 g, Fat 28 g

Sautéed Green Beans with Parmesan

Prep Time: 10 Mins, Cook Time: 5 Mins, Servings: 2

¾ lb fresh green beans (stem ends trimmed)

2 tsp olive oil

1 oz. grated Parmesan cheese (¼ cup)

1. Take a large pan, heat the olive oil overheat. Cook, occasionally turning until the green beans are crisp-tender. Cooking time may vary based on the skillet's temperature, about 4-6 mins.
2. Season with salt.
3. Remove the pan from the heat and toss in the Parmesan cheese. Serve.

Nutritions

Calories: 49 kcal, Carbohydrates: 4 g, Protein: 2 g, Fats: 2g

Baked Zucchini, Spinach, and Feta Casserole

Prep Time: 10 mins, Cook Time: 45 mins, Servings: 4

2 tbsp olive oil

2 diced small zucchini

3 cups spinach baby

2 diced small yellow squash

¼ cup fat-free crumbled feta cheese

¼ cup grated low-fat parmesan cheese

¼ cup panko breadcrumbs whole-wheat

2 large egg whites

½ tsp salt kosher

2 tsp powder garlic

½ tsp black pepper ground

1 tsp basil leaves dried

1. Preheated the oven at 400F. Set aside a casserole dish sprayed using non-stick spray & ready to use.
2. Heat in a big skillet the olive oil. Once heated, add the zucchini, spinach, & yellow squash to the pan. The spinach should be wilted & the squash should be tender after approximately 5 mins of cooking. Mix well in a mixing bowl after draining off any remaining fluid.
3. Add the rest of the ingredients to the spinach mix within a bowl. Spread the ingredients evenly in the preheated casserole dish after mixing thoroughly. Cook for about 30-40 min or until a surface is light golden. Serve warm.

Nutritions

Calories 162 kcal, Carbohydrates 20 g, Protein: 6 g, Fat 8 g

Orange Glazed Roasted Carrots

Prep Time: 10 mins, Cook Time: 30 mins, Servings: 6

3 tbsp olive oil
1 tbsp maple syrup
1 zested & juiced orange
6 peeled & sliced large carrots

Nutritions

Calories 150 kcal,
Carbohydrates 14 g, Protein 1 g,
Fat 10 g

1. Set the oven temperature to 350°F.
2. In a bowl mix together orange juice, orange zest, olive oil and maple syrup.
3. Arrange the carrots in baking large pan and pour over them the orange mix. Coat them by rolled them with a spoon.
4. Bake for 40-60 min and mix them every 20 min.

Vegetarian Portobello Mushroom Fajitas

Prep Time: 20 mins, Cook Time: 08 mins, Servings: 2

2 tbsp olive oil
2 tbsp lime juice
2 cloves minced garlic
½ finely chopped jalapeno
¼ cup finely chopped cilantro
¼ tsp salt
1/8 tsp pepper
2 portobello mushrooms
2 thinly sliced bell peppers
1 sliced onion
1 avocado
8 whole-grain tortillas
15 oz. can drain black beans

Nutritions

Calories: 398 kcal,
Carbohydrates: 60 g, Protein: 10 g, Fat: 16g

1. In a large mixing bowl, mix the olive oil, garlic, salt, pepper, lime juice, jalapeño, and cilantro to make the marinade.
2. Wipe the mushrooms with a cloth. Remove the stem and take out the gills with a knife or spoon. Cut the mushrooms into half-inch thick pieces and stir them into the marinade.
3. Mix the sliced onions and bell peppers in a large bowl.
4. Toss the veggies and marinated mushrooms in a big saucepan with hot oil. Cook for approximately 8 mins or until veggies are soft.
5. Peel and pit the avocado. In a mixing bowl, mash the avocados and add a squeeze of lemon juice and a sprinkle of salt, if preferred.
6. Serve the veggies with mashed avocados and black beans in warmed tortillas.

Kale Quinoa Salad with Cranberries

Prep Time: 25 mins, Cook Time: 0 mins, Servings: 1

For Salad:

1 cup quinoa

6 cups chopped kale

15 oz. can drained chickpeas

1 cup dried cranberries

4 oz. crumbled goat cheese

½ cup sliced almonds

1 peeled and chopped avocado

For Dressing

¼ cup extra virgin olive oil

¼ cup lime juice

2 tbsp honey

1 ½ tsp Dijon mustard

¼ tsp Kosher salt

black pepper to taste

1. Rinse the quinoa and drain it. Pour water (2 cups) in a pan with quinoa and boil. Cover the top, and boil on low flame for approximately 15 mins, or until all of the water has been absorbed. Set aside to cool.
2. Prepare the dressing. Mix all of the dressing ingredients. Toss the kale with the dressing.
3. Once the quinoa has cooled, combine it with the kale, add the chickpeas, almonds, cranberries, goat cheese, and avocado in a mixing bowl. Gently mix everything together. Serve.

Nutritions

Calories 734kcal, Carbohydrates 74g, Protein: 26g, Fat 42g

Sweet and Sour Green Beans

Prep Time: 30 Mins, Cook Time: 40 Mins, Servings: 6

1 lb fresh ends trimmed green beans
3 slices of turkey bacon chopped nitrate-free
½ cup diced yellow onion
2 tbsp vinegar apple cider
2 tbsp honey
½ tsp kosher salt

Nutritions

Calories: 104 kcal, Carbohydrates 19 g, Protein 4 g, Fat: 2 g

1. Bring the water pot to your boil in a big saucepan. After 2-3 mins, add the green beans & simmer for another 2-3 mins. To prevent your beans from overcooking, quickly rinse and immerse them into cold water. Drain all the residual water when the food has cooled.
2. Cook diced bacon in a pan over medium heat. The onion should be added when the bacon is just beginning to brown, & the bacon should be crispy.
3. Mix in drained green beans. As they start to blister from the exterior, continue cooking for a few more mins. Mix honey, vinegar, & salt into the mixture. Then toss everything together until it's evenly coated. Remove from the stove & serve.

3-Ingredient Crispy Garlic Broccoli

Prep Time: 5 mins, Cook Time: 15 mins, Servings: 4

2 lb florets broccoli
5 minced garlic cloves
2 tbsp olive oil

1. Prepare your baking sheet by lining it using parchment paper & preheating the oven to 425°F.
2. Toss all ingredients together & spread them out evenly over a baking sheet. Bake the broccoli for around 15 mins, till it is crisp-tender. It's time to eat!

Nutritions

Calories: 129 kcal, Carbohydrates: 13 g, Protein: 7 g, Fat: 8 g

PART NINE

POULTRY

Hasselback Baked Caprese Chicken

Prep Time: 5 Mins, Cook Time: 25 Mins, Servings: 2

4 medium-sized chicken breasts (boneless skinless)
1 tbsp olive oil
1 log low fat mozzarella (thinly sliced)
3 plum tomatoes, thinly sliced
Salt and pepper to taste
½ cup fresh basil leaves
Balsamic glaze
½ cup of balsamic vinegar
3 tbsp of brown sugar

1. Preheat your oven to around 400F. Make horizontal incisions in chicken breast. Season the prepared chicken with pepper and salt after rubbing it with olive oil.
2. Tomatoes and mozzarella are thinly sliced and stuffed into cuts of chicken breast, followed by basil in each incision. Bake for 25 mins, or till chicken is thoroughly cooked.
3. Meanwhile, put a small saucepan on the stove, boil brown sugar and balsamic. Cook over medium heat for about 10-12 mins or until the mixture thickens achieved.
4. Remove the chicken from the oven and coat it with balsamic dressing. If preferred, top with more fresh basil. Serve the dish with a salad or other side dish.

Nutritions

Calories: 401 kcal, Carbohydrates: 14g, Protein: 34 g, Fats 23 g

Chicken with Spinach and Tomato

Prep Time: 5 Mins, Cook Time: 20 Mins, Servings: 6

2½ lb. chicken breast (skinless boneless) cut into 1" pieces
2 tbsp olive oil
Salt
2 cloves garlic minced
Ground black pepper
7 oz. baby spinach
15 oz. canned diced tomatoes
Grated parmesan cheese optional
15 oz. canned diced tomatoes

1. Place a big saucepan over medium heat and coat it with olive oil.
2. Add the garlic and chicken to the heated oil. Salt & pepper to taste.
3. Add the spinach, tomatoes, and mushrooms when the pinkish shade of chicken and the fluids run clear. Cook till the liquid has been reduced to roughly half its original volume. If necessary, season the dish.
4. If preferred, top with cheese right before serving.

Nutritions

Calories: 173 kcal, Carbohydrates: 11 g, Protein: 40g, Fats:6 g

Turkey Tacos with Refried Beans Puree

Prep Time: 21 Mins, Cook Time: 21 Mins, Servings: 8

For beans
1 cup No salt added pinto beans (rinsed and drained)
1 Clove garlic, minced
2 tbsp Cilantro, chopped
1 Clove garlic, minced

For turkey
¼ tsp Garlic powder
¼ tsp Mild chili powder
¼ tsp Cumin
½ lb Lean ground turkey
¼ tsp Paprika

1. Heat about 2 tbsp of water in a sauté pan at medium heat to prepare the beans. Put garlic in it and Sauté for 1 min, or until garlic is aromatic. Bring the chicken broth and pinto beans to a boil. Reduce the flame to medium-low and continue to cook for another 5 mins.
2. Mash the beans using a potato masher or a fork. Cook for the next 3-4 mins or until the liquid has evaporated. Remove the pan and add 2 tbsp of chopped cilantro.
3. Heat the chili powder, paprika, garlic powder, and cumin in a sauté pan to create the turkey. Allow 1 min of toasting
4. Add turkey and 2 tbsp water. Cook for about 6-8 mins. Continue stirring to break any clumps or until well cooked. To avoid drying the pan, add another 1 tbsp of water as the water evaporates.
5. Blend the beans and turkey in a food processor until pureed.

Nutritions

Calories: 68.1 kcal, Carbohydrates: 5.4 g, Protein: 10 g, Fats: 0.9 g

Baked Chicken Breast

Prep Time: 5 Mins, Cook Time: 18 Mins, Servings: 6

- 4 boneless, skinless chicken breasts
- 1 tsp dried oregano
- 1 tsp paprika
- 1 tbsp olive oil
- ½ tsp garlic powder
- Salt and pepper

Nutritions
Calories: 146 kcal, Carbohydrates: 26 g, Protein: 24 g, Fats: 4 g

1. Preheat the oven up to 450F. Use the foil to line a baking pan.
2. Drizzle oil over all sides of the chicken breasts and place them on the baking pan.
3. In a small dish, mix the paprika, oregano, garlic powder, salt and pepper.
4. Rub this mix on both sides of the chicken breast.
5. Here are the cooking times according to the size of the chicken: 5-6 oz breasts should be baked for 13-16 mins, 8 oz breasts should be baked for 16-19 mins, and 11-12 oz breasts should be baked for 22-26 mins. Check that the chicken has achieved a warmth of 165F on the inside.
6. Remove the instant pan from the oven, cover loosely with foil, and set aside for 5-10 mins before serving and slicing the chicken.

Easy Turkey Sausage with Peppers & Onions

Prep Time: 10 mins, Cook Time: 15 mins, Servings: 8

1 lb rope sausage turkey
½ tbsp oil olive
1 cup sliced green pepper
1 cup sliced yellow pepper
1 cup sliced red onion

1. Add all ingredients to a big pan and cook over medium-high heat. Stir often as you cook until the peppers & onions are just beginning to soften.
2. Serve with brown rice like a side dish.

Nutritions

Calories 363 kcal, Carbohydrates 6 g, Protein: 18 g, Fat: 30 g

Zucchini and Sausage Casserole Skillet

Prep Time: 10 mins, Cook Time: 40 mins, Servings: 4

1 tbsp butter
3 eggs beaten
3 cups grated zucchini grated
1/3 cup grated Pepper Jack cheese
1/2 cup diced red bell pepper
1/4 cup chopped onion finely
½ lb. turkey sausage

1. Heat the oven to 350F.
2. Cook the onions and zucchini in melted butter until the onions are transparent and the zucchini is tender.
3. Stir in the sausage and cook until it is thoroughly done.
4. In an oiled pan (8x8), toss the onions, zucchini, and sausage mixture.
5. In a separate pan, make the scrambled eggs and sprinkle them on the sausage.
6. Spread cheese on top and bake for 35 to 40 mins.

Nutritions

Calories: 221kcal, Carbohydrates: 6g, Protein: 19g, Fat: 14g

Turkey Sausage Egg Roll Bowl

Prep time: 15 Mins, Cook Time: 35 Mins, Servings: 4

- 1 lb turkey sausage ground
- 1 tbsp sesame oil
- 1 cup shredded carrot
- 4 cups shredded green cabbage
- 1 cup shredded red cabbage
- ½ cup sliced thin yellow onion
- 4 minced garlic cloves
- 1 tbsp minced ginger fresh
- 1 tbsp sauce soy
- ½ tsp salt kosher
- ½ tsp black pepper ground
- ¼ cup chopped green onions
- ¼ cup chopped cilantro fresh

1. Heat a big skillet over medium-high heat. Then add your turkey sausage & heat, often turning, until it is well cooked. Drain sausage of any extra fat.
2. Using a medium-sized saucepan, heat sesame oil over medium-high heat. Then add cabbage (including red cabbage), carrots, onions, soy sauce, garlic, ginger, & salt/pepper to the sausage. It should take 3-4 mins of cooking for the cabbage to wilt but not completely lose its crisp.
3. Toss in green onions & cilantro before serving.

Nutritions

Calories 255 kcal, Carbohydrates 12 g, Protein: 24 g, Fat: 13 g

PART TEN
PORK, BEEF & LAMB

One Pan Apple Cinnamon Pork Chops

Prep Time: 15 Mins, Cook Time: 25 Mins, Servings: 6

12 oz pork chops boneless lean
½ tsp salt kosher
¼ tsp clove minced
2 tbsp olive oil extra virgin
2 sliced green apples
1 sliced yellow onion
¼ cup vegetable broth or chicken broth
1 tsp cinnamon
1 tbsp honey

1. Pat pork chops dry using a paper towel after rinsing them in cold water. Use salt & minced cloves to season all sides.
2. On moderate flame, add some olive oil to a medium-sized skillet. Add the pork chops when the pan is heated. Pork chops should be cooked thoroughly and lightly browned on all sides. Place on a cooling rack.
3. Using the same pan, sauté the apples & onion inside the leftover oil until soft. Add broth & cinnamon, then cook for some more minutes. Bring the mixture to a boil. Maintain a high flame and cook till the liquid is gone. Combine the honey, pork chops, & mustard.
4. Serve!

Nutritions

Calories 279 kcal, Carbohydrates 18g, Protein: 18 g, Fat: 15 g

Blackberry Ginger Pork Chops

Prep Time: 10 Mins, Cook Time: 40 Mins, Servings: 4

1 cup of blackberries
1 tbsp fresh grated ginger
2 tbsp honey
¼ cup water
½ tsp kosher salt
¼ tsp cinnamon
1 juiced & zested lemon
1 tbsp oil olive
4 center-cut pork chops
1 tsp garlic minced
¼ tsp black pepper ground
½ cup broth chicken

Nutritions

Calories: 298 kcal, Carbohydrates: 16 g, Protein: 30 g, Fat: 13g

1. On a moderate flame in a small saucepot, combine blackberries, salt, cinnamon, ginger, honey, lemon juice & zest. Cook for around 15-20 mins, after bringing to a boil, stirring often.
2. While your sauce is simmering, heat a pan in a medium heat with some olive oil. Seal pork chops for five minutes from each side after seasoning with garlic & pepper.
3. Reduce the heat, add broth, and then cover to complete cooking, approximately 10-15 Minutes. Make sure the chops are roasted completely but not overdone after 7-8 Mins. Is required a minimum internal temp of 145F. Serve with a of blackberry ginger sauce.

Pork with Onions and Capers

Prep time: 10 minutes, Cook time: 10 minutes, Serves 4

1 pound pork tenderloin
Butter-flavored cooking spray
1½ cups thinly sliced onion
½ cup dry vermouth
¼ cup water
2 teaspoons concentrated chicken broth
2 tablespoons capers
¼ cup fat-free sour cream
Salt and pepper, to taste

Nutritions
Calories 218 kcal,
Carbohydrates 9g,
Protein: 26 g, Fat: 6 g

1. Slice tenderloin into ½-inch slices.
2. In a large nonstick skillet, heat cooking spray over medium-high heat until hot but not smoking. Sauté pork for about 2 minutes on each side, then remove from pan.
3. Re-spray pan and add onion. Cook, stirring, for 3 to 4 minutes, or until onion just starts to brown.
4. Add vermouth and water and simmer for 3 to 4 minutes, or until liquid is reduced to about ¼ cup.
5. Stir in concentrated chicken broth and capers. Increase heat to high and bring onion mixture to a boil, then cook until reduced by half.
6. Turn off heat, stir in sour cream, and add sliced pork and any accumulated meat juices back to skillet. Turn pork slices to coat, and serve. Salt and pepper, to taste.

Skinny Cheeseburger Boats

Prep Time: 15 mins, Cook Time: 25 mins, Servings: 12

1 lb lean beef ground
1 diced onion small
½ tsp salt sea
½ tsp pepper black
3 medium bell peppers
2/3 cup divided ketchup
1 tbsp mustard
5 bars of reduced-fat cheddar cheese

Nutritions
Calories: 237 kcal,
Carbohydrates: 9 g,
Protein: 18 g, Fat: 15 g

1. Preheat the oven to 375°F.
2. Slice every bell pepper vertically six times, starting at the indentation and working your way out. Set aside the peppers.
3. Mix all the ingredients for the meatloaf in a big bowl
4. Add the meat mixture to the peppers-boats. Baking on a parchment-covered baking pan for approximately 20 mins.
5. Top every boat with a quarter of a cheese slice, then return the boats to your oven & bake for another 5 mins, till the cheese has melted.

Low-Carb Philly Cheesesteaks

Prep Time: 10 mins, Cook Time: 10 mins, Servings: 3

½ tbsp olive oil
2 lb lean sliced sirloin steak
½ tsp salt kosher
¼ tsp black pepper ground
2 tsp oregano leaves dry
1 sliced yellow onion
1 sliced bell pepper green
1 sliced bell pepper red
8 large lettuce leaves
½ cup shredded provolone cheese
2 tbsp roughly chopped cilantro fresh

1. Heat some olive oil in a medium-sized pan and in the steak that has been seasoned both sides, with pepper and salt. Add in onions, red and green bell peppers. Depending on the thickness of the beef, cook for 5-10 mins, or unless the meat is cooked thru, and the vegetables are softened.
2. Use the lettuce as cups and fill it with the mix of steak, peppers and onions. Sprinkle with cheese. Add cilantro if you like it. Serve it hot!

Nutritions

Calories 319 kcal, Carbohydrates 7 g, Protein: 29 g, Fat: 19 g

Easy Oven-Baked Meatballs

Prep Time: 15 Mins, Cook Time: 30 Mins, Servings: 3

1 lb lean beef ground
½ cup whole-wheat breadcrumbs panko
1 large egg
½ tsp salt kosher
½ tsp black pepper ground
1 tsp garlic powder
¼ cup minced yellow onion
½ tsp dried oregano
½ tsp dried basil
1 tsp oil olive

1. Set the oven temperature to 400F. Coat the baking sheet using a nonstick spray.
2. In a large bowl, combine all of the ingredients & thoroughly mix them. Form the meatball into 1" balls, then put on the baking sheet.
3. Bake for 20 minutes.
4. Add the meatballs at your whole wheat pasta and enjoy.

Nutritions

Calories 145 kcal, Carbohydrates 5 g, Protein: 18 g, Fat: 5g

PART ELEVEN
FISH & SEAFOOD

Salmon Salad

Prep Time: 20 Mins, Cook Time: 16 Mins, Servings: 4

Salmon
1½ tbsp olive oil
4 salmon fillets (about 1 lb)

Honey Mustard Dressing
2 tbsp honey
3 tbsp olive oil
1 tbsp apple cider vinegar
1 ½ tbsp Dijon mustard
pepper (to taste)
Kosher salt

Salad
4 cups spinach
1 cup walnuts
1 cup low fat goat cheese
1 cup blueberries
1 cup avocado
¾ cup diced onion

1. Preheat your oven to 400 F. Line a baking dish with parchment paper. Place the salmon in the baking dish (skin side down). Rub olive oil over the fish and season with pepper and salt. Bake the salmon for about 12-18 mins, or until the thickest portion reaches 145°F temperature. Allow salmon to cool slightly before serving.

2. Blend the olive oil, Dijon mustard, honey, and cider vinegar until smooth. Season with salt and pepper.

3. In large salad dish, add spinach, walnut, red onion, avocado, goat cheese, and blueberries. Serve with cooked salmon on top.

Nutritions
Calories: 767 kcal, Carbohydrates: 26 g, Protein: 44 g, Fats: 57 g

Tuna Zucchini Noodle Bake

Prep Time: 10 mins, Cook Time: 20 mins, Servings: 6

4 medium zucchinis spiralized
2 tsp olive oil
½ cup diced yellow onions
12 oz drained tuna cans
1 tbsp paste tomato
15 oz drained diced tomatoes
½ cup low fat milk skim
1 tsp dried thyme
½ tsp kosher salt
¼ tsp black pepper ground
¼ cup grated parmesan cheese
½ cup of cheddar cheese shredded fat-free

1. Spray a pan using nonstick spray and heat the oven to 400°F. In a casserole dish, evenly distribute the zucchini. Set aside.

2. Heat oil in a big pan, then add chopped onion & cook for 2 mins. Add the tuna & tomato paste and cook for another minute. Add the diced tomato, milk, thyme, salt & pepper to taste. Stir the parmesan and bring to simmer.

3. Put the mix on top the zucchini, sprinkle with cheddar cheese, and bake for 15 minutes, or until the cheese is melted.

Nutritions
Calories: 164 kcal, Carbohydrates: 10 g, Protein: 18 g, Fat: 7 g

Curried Coconut Mussels

Prep Time: 10 mins, Cook Time: 20 mins, Servings: 6

2 tbsp water

½ cup diced yellow onion

½ cup diced bell pepper

3 minced garlic cloves

½ tsp black pepper ground

2 tbsp powder curry

1 cup low fat milk coconut

½ cup broth vegetable

2 lb washed & cleaned mussels

¼ cup chopped cilantro fresh

1. In a big pan over medium heat add the bell pepper, onion, garlic and the 2 tbsp of water. Salt & pepper to taste.
2. Toss in the curry powders, hot peppers, coconut low fat milk, & veggie broth. To avoid curry powder lumps in the soup, whisk everything together well. Add your mussels to the simmering mixture. When all the mussels have opened, cover & simmer for 5-6 mins, or till they're done cooking. Unopened mussels should be thrown away.
3. Serve in individual serving dishes with some chopped cilantro on top. Serve with brown rice & quinoa if preferred.

Nutritions

Calories 331 kcal Carbohydrates 15g, Protein: 29 g, Fat: 18 g

Mediterranean Chopped Salad with Salmon, Cucumber, and Mint

Prep Time: 10 mins, Cook Time: 10 mins, Servings: 3

2 cups roughly chopped romaine lettuce

2 chopped small tomatoes

1 chopped small cucumber

1 chopped small bell pepper

¼ cup chopped small parsley fresh

2 tbsp chopped small mint fresh

1 tbsp juice lemon

2 tsp zest lemon

24 oz filets salmon

½ tsp salt kosher

¼ tsp black pepper ground

1. If you don't have a broiler, preheat your oven to 500F.
2. Toss the romaine lettuce with the radishes and the rest of the ingredients in a large salad bowl. Toss well & put away.
3. Place the salmon fillets on a baking pan that has been sprayed with nonstick spray. Salt & pepper to taste. Cook for approximately 10 mins over the oven broiler, till the top, is gently browned & the meat is cooked through. Halfway through the cooking time, check your salmon & move the pan if necessary to get an equal browning.
4. To serve, divide the salad among serving dishes and top with the salmon. Top the salmon with the lemon zest.

Nutritions

Calories: 390 kcal, Carbohydrates: 8 g, Protein: 36 g, Fat: 23 g

Avocado Tuna Salad

Prep Time: 10 Mins, Cook Time: 10 Mins, Servings: 2

12 oz light tuna canned chunk
1 mashed avocado
1 chopped red onion
1 cup chopped celery
1 chopped tomato medium
1 juiced lemon
1 tbsp extra virgin olive oil
½ tsp chili flakes red
½ tsp salt
½ tsp black pepper ground

1. Mix all ingredients in a wide bowl.
2. Enjoy.

Nutritions
Calories: 240 kcal, Carbohydrates: 12 g, Protein: 24 g, Fat: 12g

Blackened Sockeye Salmon

Prep Time: 5 Mins, Cook Time: 15 Mins, Servings: 2

12 oz salmon fillets sockeye
2 tbsp divided olive oil
Spices Blackened
1 tbsp thyme dried
2 tsp powder garlic
1 tbsp oregano dried
1 tbsp paprika
1 tbsp pepper black
1 tsp pepper cayenne
sea salt kosher

1. Add the spices to a medium bowl and mix well.
2. Coat all sides of salmon with olive oil. Season the fish evenly.
3. Toss the salmon with oil in a pan and cook over medium-high heat.
4. Cook the salmon on medium-low, for about 5-6 mins on all sides. The salmon must flake readily using a fork & the skin must be crispy.

Nutritions
Calories: 260 kcal, Carbohydrates: 4 g, Protein: 19 g, Fat: 19g

Orange Miso Wild Cod Recipe

Prep Time: 5 Mins, Cook Time: 18 Mins, Servings: 1

24 oz wild skinless cod fillet

2 tbsp mellow white miso paste

¼ cup soy sauce low sodium

1 tbsp maple syrup

1 zested & juiced navel orange

1 tbsp ginger paste minced ginger

1. Set the oven temperature to 375°F.
2. Combine navel orange zest and juice, soy sauce, miso paste, maple syrup, and chopped ginger in a large mixing bowl & stir until well combined.
3. Add some cooking spray to a baking sheet and add the fish.
4. Apply the miso glaze to the fish.
5. Cook for 10-15 mins in a 375F oven.
6. Increase oven temp to a high broil. Check every 2 to 3 mins to make sure you don't overheat.
7. When the glaze has browned, and the fish is flaky, it's ready to be served.

Nutritions

Calories: 200 kcal, Carbohydrates: 12 g, Protein: 32 g, Fat: 2g

Crab and Corn Salad

Prep Time: 10 Mins, Cook Time: 5 Mins, Servings: 2

8 oz meat crab

8 oz kernels corn

1 sliced thin Fresno chili

¼ cup chopped fine bell pepper green

¼ cup chopped fine green onion

½ tsp powder chili

¼ tsp ground cumin

2 tbsp chopped cilantro fresh

1 juiced & zested navel orange

1 juiced & zested lime

1. Mix all of the ingredients well. Allow the flavors to meld for 5 mins before serving.
2. Serve at room temperature.

Nutritions

Calories: 82 kcal, Carbohydrates: 12 g, Protein: 8 g, Fat: 1g

Sriracha Salmon Power Bowl

Prep Time: 10 Mins, Cook Time: 40 Mins, Servings: 1

½ tbsp oil olive
6 oz skinless salmon
2 tsp Seasoning Old Bay
½ cup cubed sweet potatoes
½ tsp salt Kosher
¼ cup broth chicken
¼ cup shredded carrots
¼ cup of broccoli
¼ cup of arugula
½ cup of spinach
1 tbsp sriracha
1 wedges lime
1 tbsp chopped cilantro fresh

1. Set the oven temperature to 375 degrees. Rub olive oil & Bay Seasoning on the fish before cooking. Roast for around 18 to 22 mins, or unless crisp & flaky, in a medium baking dish.
2. Sprinkle the sweet potato cubes with leftover olive oil & salt in a baking dish during the salmon's roasting. Bake at 375°F for 20 to 25 mins, unless the sweet potatoes become soft but not mush. Remove from the oven and let cool before serving.
3. The nonstick skillet should be preheated to medium heat. Toss in some broccoli, carrots, & a quarter cup of chicken or veggie stock. Cook for around 5 mins or until they're tender.
4. Divide your baby arugula & baby spinach into 2 serving dishes and toss them together with the lemon juice. Sauteed veggies and sweet potatoes should be layered on top. Top each dish with skinless salmon. Serve with lime wedges, cilantro, & sriracha chili sauce drizzled over the top.

Nutritions

Calories: 216 kcal, Carbohydrates: 15 g, Protein: 19 g, Fat: 9g

Fast and Flavorful Chimichurri Shrimp

Prep Time: 5 Mins, Cook Time: 5 Mins, Servings: 1

2 cups fresh parsley
¼ cup fresh oregano
3 cloves garlic
½ tsp chili flakes red
2 tsp vinegar red wine
1/3 cup + 1 tbsp oil olive
1 tsp salt kosher
2 lb peeled & deveined shrimp large

1. Add the oregano, garlic, chili flakes, and parsley into a food processor. Pulse until the mixture is finely minced. Add vinegar & half of the salt and pulse again until incorporated into the mixture. Add gradually 1/3 cup of olive oil until well-combined.
2. Set the broiler to a low setting. Mix the remaining salt & olive oil with the shrimp.
3. Then broil for approximately 5 Mins until the shrimps are cooked through. Remove from the oven and mix with chimichurri sauce before serving.

Nutritions

Calories: 268 kcal, Carbohydrates: 2 g, Protein: 32 g, Fat: 14g

Seared Tuna with Wasabi Cream

Prep Time: 10 Mins, Cook Time: 30 Mins, Servings: 1 steak

1 tbsp oil olive
24 oz steaks tuna
¼ cup sauce ponzu
1 tbsp paste wasabi
1 tbsp water
2 tsp minced fresh ginger
1 tbsp cream coconut
2 tsp aminos coconut

1. Marinate the tuna for about 10 mins in ponzu sauce.
2. In a pan, heat olive oil to medium-high heat. Sear the tuna for 3 mins on all sides. After cooking, the core of the tuna would remain pink.
3. In a mixing bowl, mix the rest of the ingredients until they form a smooth mixture. Drizzled the tuna with the sauce.

Nutritions

Calories: 298 kcal, Carbohydrates: 2 g, Protein: 40 g, Fat: 13g

PART TWELVE

DESSERT

Flourless Blueberry Oatmeal Muffins

Prep Time: 15 Mins, Cook Time: 25 Mins, Servings: 10

2 & ½ cups rolled oats old-fashioned

1 & ½ cups of low fat milk almond

1 lightly beaten large egg

1/3 cup maple syrup

2 tbsp melted coconut oil

1 tsp extract vanilla

1 tsp ground cinnamon

1 tsp baking powder

¼ tsp salt

1 tsp grated lemon zest

1 cup fresh blueberries

1. In a medium bowl, mix both oats & almond low fat milk. Cover & refrigerate overnight.
2. Set the oven temperature to 375°F. Spray a nonstick spray the muffin pan.
3. Stir all the other ingredients into your soaked oats to mix. Fill your muffin tin approximately ¾ of the way with the batter.
4. About 20 mins in the oven, or until the tops are browned. Enjoy it warm.

Nutritions

Calories: 122 kcal, Carbohydrates: 19 g, Protein: 3 g, Fat: 4 g

3-Ingredient Vanilla Frosting

Prep Time: 5 mins, Cook Time: 5 mins, Servings: 16

8 oz reduced-fat cream cheese

¼ cup of honey

1 tsp vanilla pure

1. In a large bowl, combine all of the ingredients & beat for 3-5 mins.
2. Please keep it in the fridge until you're ready to use it over the cupcake.

Nutritions

Calories: 53 kcal, Carbohydrates: 4 g, Protein: 1 g, Fat: 4 g

Healthy Apple Cake Muffins

Prep Time: 12 mins, Cook Time: 15-20 mins, Servings: 12

4 tbsp unsalted butter
1/2 cup honey/pure maple syrup
1/2 cup unsweetened applesauce
1/2 cup plain nonfat Greek yogurt
1/4 cup low fat milk
2 large eggs
1 tsp vanilla extract
1 tsp baking soda
1/2 tsp baking powder
1/2 tsp salt
1 1/2 tsp cinnamon
1 ½ cups whole wheat flour
1 ½ cup large, chopped baking apple

1. Heat the oven to 350F. Coat standard or small muffin tins with cooking spray.
2. Melt the butter in the microwave at a high temperature in a bowl.
3. In the same dish as the butter, combine the low fat milk, applesauce, eggs, honey/maple syrup, plain nonfat Greek yogurt, and vanilla extract. Whisk everything together until it's smooth.
4. Toss in the salt, cinnamon, baking soda, and baking powder with the prepared wet Ingredients in the mixing bowl. Whisk everything together until it's smooth.
5. Finally, stir in the whole white wheat flour until it's nearly thoroughly mixed.
6. Stir in the diced apple, keeping a few bits for the muffin tops if preferred. Mix in the apple with the rubber spatula until everything is well mixed.
7. Spoon the mixture into the oiled muffin tins and place the apple bits on top.
8. Bake for 16 to 18 mins, or until a toothpick inserted in the middle comes out clean.
9. Cool for 10 mins in the pan before transferring to a cooling rack.
10. Serve them right away or store them for up to 3 days in the freezer.

Nutritions

Calories: 134 kcal, Carbohydrates: 22 g, Protein: 4 g, Fat: 4g

Apple Cinnamon Cookie Energy Bites

Prep Time: 20 mins, Cook Time: 0 mins, Servings: 2 dozen

2 cups simple oats
¼ cup crushed flaxseed
¾ tsp cinnamon
½ cup almond butter
¼ cup+1 tbsp maple syrup
1 tsp vanilla extract
pinch of salt
1 cup grated apple

1. Combine the flaxseeds, oats, and cinnamon in a large mixing basin. Add the maple syrup, vanilla, almond butter, and sprinkle of salt in a separate dish or liquid measuring cup and mix until well blended. Pour the oat mixture over it and stir until it is uniformly covered. Add the grated apple and mix well.
2. With the help of a cookie scoop, divide the mixture into tbsp-sized parts and roll it into a ball with your palms (damp your hands to avid stickiness).
3. Serve them right away or keep the energy bites refrigerated inside an airtight container for 3-4 days. Enjoy!

Nutritions

Calories 161kcal, Carbohydrates 19g, Protein: 5g, Fat: 8g

Healthy Carrot Cake Muffins

Prep Time: 15 Mins, Cook Time: 15 Mins, Servings: 4

2 eggs
1 cup unsweetened applesauce
¼ cup melted unsalted butter
½ cup pure maple syrup
½ tsp salt
1 tsp baking soda
1 tsp cinnamon
¼ tsp ground nutmeg
2 tsp vanilla extract
¼ tsp ground ginger
1 ½ cups of whole wheat flour
1 ½ cups peeled grated carrot
¼ tsp ground cloves

1. Preheat the oven up to 350F. Line the muffin pans using paper liners or cooking spray.
2. Beat the eggs, maple syrup, and applesauce in a large mixing dish. Take a separate bowl to whisk the melted butter and egg yolks together.
3. Whisk together the cinnamon, baking soda, cloves, salt, nutmeg, ginger, and vanilla till a smooth mixture form.
4. Gently mix the oats, wheat flour, and grated carrot using a spatula. Make sure the batter isn't over-mixed. It will become a thick batter.
5. Fill all muffin cups for ¾ with the batter, dividing the 12 muffin cups equally. Bake for 18 to 20 mins, till a toothpick inserted in the middle of a muffin, turns clean.
6. Allow 5 mins for the muffins to cool before transferring to a wire rack.

Nutritions

Calories: 174 kcal, Carbohydrates: 28 g, Protein: 4 g, Fats: 6 g

Maple Coffee Ice Pops

Prep Time: 5 Mins, Cook time: 8 hrs, Servings: 4

3 tbsp maple syrup

1 & ½ cup strong black coffee

1 tsp ground cinnamon

1 cup low fat coconut cream

1. Mix all the ingredients.
2. Pour on popsicle molds.
3. To freeze, insert one popsicle stick.
4. Put in the fridge overnight till it is completely firm.

Nutritions

Calories: 160 kcal, Carbohydrates: 10 g, Protein: 2 g, Fat: 14g

Chocolate Hummus Fruit Dip

Prep Time: 5 Mins, Cook Time: 5 Mins, Servings: 2

1 & ½ cups drained garbanzo beans

2 tbsp tahini

2 tbsp syrup maple

4 tbsp cocoa powder unsweetened

1 tsp extract vanilla

1. In your food processor, mix all ingredients. Blend until completely smooth. Add some warm water if the mixture becomes too thick.
2. To serve, top with fresh fruit.

Nutritions

Calories: 70 kcal, Carbohydrates: 10 g, Protein: 3 g, Fat: 3g

Chocolate Raspberry Truffles

Prep Time: 10 Mins, Cook time: 0 Min, Servings: 12 Truffle

Truffles

1 cup frozen raspberries

1 cup unsalted walnuts raw

½ cup desiccated coconut

6 pitted Medjool dates

3 tbsp cocoa powder

1 tsp vanilla extract

¼ tsp salt

Outer Coating

½ cup desiccated coconut

3 tbsp freeze-dried raspberries

1. In your food processor, combine all truffle ingredients & pulse until smooth.
2. Place the 1" balls over a baking sheet that has been lined with parchment paper.
3. Refrigerate for fifteen to thirty minutes.
4. Meantime, in a food processor, mix the ingredients for the outer coating & pulse 2 to 3 times or unless the coconut becomes pink.
5. Take the truffles out of the fridge and roll each one in the coating.
6. Re-chill in the fridge for approximately three hours.

Nutritions

Calories: 144 kcal, Carbohydrates: 17 g, Protein: 2 g, Fat: 9g

Baked Apple Chips

Prep Time: 10 Mins, Cook Time: 2 hrs, Servings: 4

2 thinly sliced apples cored

cinnamon

1. Make sure the oven is preheated at 275F.
2. Place the sliced apples on a parchment-lined cookie sheet.
3. Add a dash of cinnamon on top (to taste).
4. Bake for 2 hours. After the first 60 Mins, rotate every slice to ensure equal cooking. To avoid overcooking them, you must check after 60 mins & every 30 mins after that.
5. Remove these from your oven after they've browned and crisped up to your liking.

Nutritions

Calories: 32 kcal, Carbohydrates: 8.5 g, Protein: 12 g, Fat: 7 g

PART THIRTEEN
STAPLES & SAUCES

Oil-Free Pesto

Prep Time: 5 mins, Cook Time: 0 mins, Servings: 4

2 cups spinach
¼ cup low fat parmesan cheese
3 diced garlic cloves
¼ cup freshly squeezed lemon juice
salt

1. In a food processor, mix all the ingredients & pulse till a pesto-like consistency is achieved.
2. Keep chilled until you're ready to serve.

Nutritions

Calories: 23 kcal, Carbohydrates: 2 g, Protein: 2 g, Fat: 1 g

Greek Yogurt Onion Dip

Prep time: 5 minutes, Cook time: 0 mins, Makes about 1 cup

1 cup plain nonfat Greek yogurt
1 (28-gram) packet dried onion soup mix
Freshly ground black pepper

1. In a small bowl, combine the Greek yogurt with the onion soup mix and whisk well to combine.
2. Season with black pepper. Serve immediately or cover and refrigerate to serve cold. To store, refrigerate in an airtight container for up to 1 week.

Nutritions

Calories: 53 kcal, Carbohydrates: 7 g, Protein: 6 g, Fat: 0 g

Rainbow Salsa Recipe

Prep Time: 10 mins, Cook Time: 10 mins, Servings: 5

2 diced small tomatoes
1 habanero minced pepper small
1 diced small bell pepper yellow
¼ cup chopped cilantro fresh
1 diced small red onion
1 tbsp juice lime
1 tsp kosher salt
14 oz drained & rinsed black beans

1. Mix all of the ingredients well together before serving. Wait a few mins until serving to allow the flavors to meld.

Nutritions

Calories: 79 kcal, Carbohydrates: 15 g, Protein: 5 g, Fat: 0 g

Macadamia Date Butter

Prep Time: 3 Mins, Cook Time: 0 Mins, Servings: 4

1 & 1/3 cup of nuts macadamia

2/3 cups of pitted dates

1 cup of low fat milk almond

1. In your food processor, combine the nuts & dates. Make hummus-like consistency by adding some almond low fat milk & blending until it's smooth.

Nutritions

Calories: 100 kcal, Carbohydrates: 6 g, Protein: 1 g, Fat: 9 g

Easy Plant-Based Mayonnaise Recipe

Prep Time: 10 Mins, Cook Time: 10 Mins, Servings: 2 cup

1 cup of cashews
¾ cup of water
2 tbsp vinegar white
2 tbsp freshly squeezed lemon juice
1 tsp powder garlic
½ tsp powder onion
½ tsp salt
½ tsp Mustard Dijon
¼ tsp paprika

1. Combine all ingredients in a blender until they reach the desired consistency.
2. Refrigerate in an airtight container for at least 8 hrs before serving. This will give the mayo enough time to stiffen before serving.

Nutritions
Calories: 46 kcal, Carbohydrates: 3 g, Protein: 2 g, Fat: 4g

Made in United States
Troutdale, OR
04/16/2024

19229598R00053